ZADIE'S SHOES

ADAM PETTLE

Zadie's Shoes
first published 2001 by
Scirocco Drama
An imprint of J. Gordon Shillingford Publishing Inc.
© 2001 Adam Pettle

Scirocco Drama Series Editor: Glenda MacFarlane
Cover design by Doowah Design Inc.
Author photo by Geneviève Steele
Back cover photo taken by Heather Morton and features Kelli Fox and Jordan Pettle
from the original Factory Theatre production.
Printed and bound in Canada

Many thanks to Lillian Butovsky and Ellie Hoidel for proofreading the Yiddish.

We acknowledge the financial assistance of the Manitoba Arts Council and
The Canada Council for the Arts for our publishing program.

Canadian Cataloguing in Publication Data

Pettle, Adam, 1973-
    Zadie's Shoes

A play.
ISBN 1-896239-78-1

    I. Title.

PS8581.E858Z33 2001   C812'.6   C2001-900238-6
PR9199.3.P455Z33 2001

J. Gordon Shillingford Publishing
P.O. Box 86, 905 Corydon Avenue, Winnipeg, MB Canada R3M 3S3

To my Zadies and Bubies
Abe, Roy, Shush and Ruth.

Adam Pettle

Adam Pettle was born and raised in Toronto. His first play, *Therac 25* (Scirocco Drama, 2000), has received numerous productions across Canada and will be revived in Toronto in the spring of 2002 at the Factory Theatre. Adam is currently working on several new projects including *Sunday Father*, a new play co-commissioned by the Canadian Stage Company and the Royal Exchange Theatre in Manchester, England, and *Misha*, a play for young audiences commissioned by Theatre Direct Canada, which will premiere at Theatre Passe Muraille in 2002.

Zadie's Shoes, which was the smash-hit of Factory Theatre's 2000/01 season, was picked up by Mirvish Productions and will open at Toronto's Wintergarden Theatre in March 2002.

Production Credits

Zadie's Shoes was first produced at the Factory Theatre in Toronto, Ontario, in January, 2001, with the following cast:

SEAN	Paul Essiembre
RUTH	Kelli Fox
BETH	Torri Higginson
BEAR	Randy Hughson
LILY	Juno Mills-Cockell
BENJAMIN	Jordan Pettle
ELI/JACOB	Paul Soles

Directed by Jackie Maxwell
Set and costume design by Sue LePage
Lighting design by Robert Thomson
Original Music and Sound design by Marc Desormeaux
Stage Manager: Beatrice Campbell
Apprentice Stage Manager: Holly Korhonen
Produced by David Baile and Ken Gass

Special thanks to Wayne Beaver, Christine Brubaker, Deanna Brown, Canadian Stage Company, Henry Gilbert, Patty Gilbert, Mark Milliere, Ryerson Theatre, Flo Short, National Ballet of Canada, Sportsdesk, Tarragon Theatre, Theatre Passe Muraille, Toronto Curling Club, and the Young People's Theatre.

Notes to Pronunciation

From its beginnings, the Yiddish language has been written using letters of the Hebrew alphabet. To reach readers unfamiliar with that alphabet, writers have transcribed the Yiddish words with transliterations that often varied from writer to writer. In this text, we have used the standard established by the Yivo Institute for Jewish Research. The pronunciation of most letters will be readily apparent. The folowing table should help with those that are not:

Transliteration	English Equivalent
tsh	As in **"chip"**
kh	As in "Ba**ch**" or "lo**ch**"
a	As in "m**a**"
o	As in "**for**"
u	As in "b**oo**k"
e	As in "m**e**t". Please note that the letter "e" is always pronounced. (There is no silent "e" in English.) So, for example, the word "rebe" is pronounced with two syllables: re-be.
ey	As in "d**ay**"
ay	As in "f**i**ne"
oy	As in "b**oy**"
i	Somewhere between "m**ee**t" and "m**i**tt" in length and tenseness.

There are no double letters. So, for example, the Yiddish word for "bum" or "hanger-on" is written "shleper" and not as you might sometimes see it "shlepper."

The word "zadie" in the title remains as it originally appeared in the production of the play.

We have used an apostrophe to indicate a vowel said so quickly as to be imperceptible. Thus a cry for help can be pronounced "gevald" or when the first vowel is barely heard "g'vald."

Prologue

The lights come up on ELI, a man in his seventies.

ELI: There was a man who dreamt all night of the number eight. He woke at exactly eight o'clock in the morning only to realize that it was the eighth day of August, the eighth month. He looked out his window to see eight beautiful birds sitting on a wire outside of his room singing to him. He rose, showered for eight minutes, hopped on the number eight bus and rode all the way down eighth avenue to the track. He waited. And at exactly eight minutes before the eighth race he put eight hundred dollars, his entire life savings, on the number eight horse to win. The eight horse was a gray mare out of California who went off at odds of eight-to-one. The race went off miraculously at eight minutes to the hour. And as the sun set and the horses charged down the backstretch anyone who's ever spent a day in their life searching for a sign can tell you what happened: the horse finished eighth.

Act One

Scene 1

A one-bedroom apartment. Tuesday night.

> *RUTH, a woman in her late twenties, is lying in bed.*
> *She is looking through a pamphlet from the*
> *"American Biologers Wellness Clinic" while*
> *BENJAMIN, a man in his late twenties, sits beside*
> *her staring intently at the television.*

RUTH: Cafeina. What's coffee in Spanish? Is it cafeina?
            Boo?

BENJAMIN: Sorry, I didn't... I was just...

RUTH: We should've never got cable in here.

BENJAMIN: It was your idea.

RUTH: Yes, so I'd have something to do in between
            retching...not to mark the end of any future
            communication in our bedroom.

BENJAMIN: I just need to see if the Argos won and then I am all
            yours.

RUTH: The Argos? Since when do you...since when does
            anybody care about the Argos?

BENJAMIN: Come on, it's a big game. If they win they'll make
            the playoffs. They'll be four and nine but they'll
            make the playoffs.

RUTH:	This is not football, this is large Scottish men carrying telephone poles.
BENJAMIN:	*Sportsdesk* is on in two minutes.
RUTH:	I can't wait. Boo?
BENJAMIN:	Hmm?
RUTH:	Do we have an investment in this game?
BENJAMIN:	No.
RUTH:	Benjamin?
BENJAMIN:	What?
RUTH:	Promise me.
BENJAMIN:	We don't…we've discussed…that's over.
RUTH:	Right. I wonder if there'll be anything on Beth.
BENJAMIN:	What?
RUTH:	On *Sportsdesk*.
BENJAMIN:	They may do a preview of Regina.
RUTH:	I can't believe it's here already, her big day is Friday… Just like two other people I know, if someone ever remembers to pick up the tickets.
BENJAMIN:	Tomorrow.
RUTH:	You were supposed to do it—
BENJAMIN:	They're not going anywhere.
RUTH:	The last of my money has been sitting on that table for—
BENJAMIN:	It's collecting interest.
RUTH:	Speaking of interest.
BENJAMIN:	Hmm?

RUTH:	How about showing me some?
BENJAMIN:	I'm here. I'm with you.
RUTH:	No, you're...I can't believe I'm losing out to—he's pulling a truck.
BENJAMIN:	Yes.
RUTH:	With his teeth! Aww Boo, will you turn this drek off please?
BENJAMIN:	One minute.
RUTH:	Oh, look at that—we have ourselves a winner. Look at him, he's going crazy, his tits are jiggling all over the—
BENJAMIN:	He's just been named the world's strongest power stepper.
RUTH:	Don't you hold that title?
BENJAMIN:	That's power shleper.
RUTH:	I wish I was there when she won.
BENJAMIN:	You were a little busy.
RUTH:	Do you think we should be going to Regina instead of Mexico?
BENJAMIN:	Is that a trick question?
RUTH:	No, I'm... Do you realize I haven't even seen her since she won?
BENJAMIN:	You'll see her tomorrow.
RUTH:	Yeah. And God only knows what she's going to do when I tell her... Actually that's not true. I know exactly what she's going to do, which is why I can't...I'm going to wait.
BENJAMIN:	What are you going to do? Get on the plane and let

them wonder where you are for the next two months?

RUTH: That's not a bad idea.

BENJAMIN: You're not leaving without telling them.

RUTH: I'm going to totally ruin her concentration, she'll probably lose the whole thing just because I'm going to throw this in her face two days before the biggest tournament of her—

BENJAMIN: That's wise, blame yourself.

RUTH: You know how she feels about anything alternative, she won't even use margarine. And Lily, how am I going to...? She couldn't handle when I was in isolation for three days, how is she going to manage—?

BENJAMIN: She'll manage.

RUTH: I'm the only person she can talk to.

BENJAMIN: I've got an idea: why don't you stop worrying about everybody else and start worrying about yourself.

RUTH: That's very insightful.

BENJAMIN: They're your sisters.

RUTH: Exactly! Do you remember the last time we all sat down for lunch?

BENJAMIN: No, was it a little tense?

RUTH: The last supper was a little tense, this meal was beyond tense. You remember—it was Beth's birthday, I was in the middle of my first cycle of chemo, Lily was thinking about moving to Papua New Guinea.

BENJAMIN: Right.

RUTH:	Christ, I'm sure they haven't spoken since. I just...I can't handle it...not tomorrow...I really can't handle the Hindenberg.
BENJAMIN:	Are you going to be OK in a restaurant?
RUTH:	We'll see.
BENJAMIN:	That's comforting.
RUTH:	I'm going crazy locked up in here. I'll go right there and come right home.
BENJAMIN:	Do you want me to call in sick and come with you?
RUTH:	No, work. You've got to work. Besides you've got a million things to do to get us ready. You've got to do laundry, pick up the tickets and...you're right...I mean I know you're right...I've just got to tell them already. I don't want to have to think about it anymore.

> *The theme song to "Sportsdesk" plays and BENJAMIN's attention shifts to the television.*

Jesus, you're like Pavlov's dog with that song.

| BENJAMIN: | One score. |

> *Pause.*

RUTH:	Did you remember to cancel the paper? Boo?
BENJAMIN:	Just... *(He holds out a hand to say "one minute.")*
RUTH:	Right. Enema *Cafeina*...you know I've met tons of people that have done it but I still...I can't quite get a grasp on how spraying coffee up your ass can possibly—?
BENJAMIN:	Shit...oh no.
RUTH:	What?
BENJAMIN:	Fuck!

RUTH: What?!

BENJAMIN: Nothing…just…the Argos.

RUTH: They lost?

BENJAMIN: Forty-nine to… Fuck.

RUTH: A regular tragedy. *(Beat.)* What'd we lose?

BENJAMIN: What?

RUTH: Oh please don't just what? Twenty? Forty?

BENJAMIN: Fifty.

RUTH: Benjamin!

BENJAMIN: I know. I just… I had a feeling.

RUTH: A feeling?

BENJAMIN: Yeah, must've just been gas eh?

RUTH: I can't believe…

BENJAMIN: It was my last… It was my swan song.

RUTH: Your swan song just cost us fifty bucks.

BENJAMIIN: I know, I'm shit. I'm sorry.

RUTH: Unbelievable. Can I ?

             He nods. She turns off the television. Beat.

             So?

BENJAMIN: Hmm?

RUTH: How does coffee up the ee-ee help?

BENJAMIN: What?

RUTH: You weren't listening.

BENJAMIN: Tell me, what is it?

RUTH:			Forget it, it'll be a surprise. *Cafeina*...they make it sound so sexy...*ciao cafeina*, I wonder if anything you write will ever be translated into Spanish.

BENJAMIN:		I doubt it.

RUTH:			That's the spirit.

BENJAMIN:		I'm not a writer.

RUTH:			Oh no? What are you?

BENJAMIN:		Waiter.

RUTH:			Hey, I thought yesterday was self-deprecation day.

BENJAMIN:		It's kind of a festival.

RUTH:			Boo?

BENJAMIN:		What?

RUTH:			Nobody died. It's a football game.

BENJAMIN:		It's not the... I...I'm just wired.

RUTH:			Two more days.

BENJAMIN:		Yeah.

RUTH:			We just have to get out of here already. Our own private villa on the ocean...and yeah, Juan Valdez will be paying the occasional visit to the hut but...it'll be normal... Well, more normal than it has been for a long time. It'll be just you and me and...God, I can't remember the last time things felt normal, you?

BENJAMIN:		The early eighties.

RUTH:			Are you going to get the light?

BENJAMIN:		I'm not ready for bed. I'm going to go read.

			He moves to exit.

RUTH: Boo?

BENJAMIN: Hmm?

RUTH: Aren't you going to tell me sweet dreams?

BENJAMIN: I'm...sweet dreams.

RUTH: And luck, for tomorrow.

BENJAMIN: And luck, for tomorrow.

Scene 2

A Synagogue. Wednesday morning.

> *BENJAMIN sits beside ELI. ELI is staring at the bimah and shaking his head. The morning service has just ended.*

ELI: It's not what it used to be.

BENJAMIN: Sorry?

ELI: The temple, it's not what it used to be. This one wants money for a tree, this one wants money for Big Julie's picnic...didn't... It didn't used to be about money.

BENJAMIN: I wouldn't know.

ELI: No?

BENJAMIN: No.

ELI: *(Kissing his tallis and putting it away.)* Where's your tallis?

BENJAMIN: Oh, a...I don't have one.

ELI: Did you have a bar mitzvah?

BENJAMIN: Yes.

ELI:	The last time you were here?
BENJAMIN:	A…pretty much.
ELI:	Still, you had a bar mitzvah, you should have a tallis. You don't look Jewish.
BENJAMIN:	What?!
ELI:	You don't look Jewish.
BENJAMIN:	I couldn't look more Jewish.
ELI:	It's not such a bad thing.
BENJAMIN:	What?
ELI:	To look Jewish.
BENJAMIN:	No, it's…I never said that it—
ELI:	Why today?
BENJAMIN:	Sorry?
ELI:	Why is this day different from all other days? Why come today?
BENJAMIN:	I don't know.
ELI:	What did you just say?
BENJAMIN:	I said I don't—
ELI:	I saw this Indian on a program saying "I don't know" is the greatest prayer in the world, do you think that's right?
BENJAMIN:	I don't…maybe.
ELI:	No, not maybe! "I don't know" is not in this book. "I don't know" is not a Jewish prayer.
BENJAMIN:	A Jewish— ?
ELI:	A Jewish boy must always know!

BENJAMIN: I...I'm sorry, but I'm not so sure that's true.

ELI: No?

BENJAMIN: No.

ELI: Auschwitz. They walk you out...which line would you like to go in, Juda? Oh...I don't know, you choose. OK. *(Makes a gun with his fingers and pulls the trigger.)* So please, don't tell me I don't know.

BENJAMIN: It's just...it's kind of private.

ELI: Nothing Jewish is private. I saw you walk in, searching for something, somebody...searching for a man who could give you some answers. Where's your father?

BENJAMIN: My...?! Boston.

ELI: What's he doing there?

BENJAMIN: He's a doctor.

ELI: People don't get sick in Toronto?

BENJAMIN: He's a plastic surgeon.

ELI: People aren't farklempt and ugly in Toronto?

BENJAMIN: He got a great offer a few years ago and—

ELI: Money?

BENJAMIN: I guess.

ELI: It didn't used to be about money.

BENJAMIN: What?

ELI: Medicine.

BENJAMIN: No?

ELI: No, it was about telling everyone your son was a doctor. So, where is your father the doctor's father?

A zadie's advice is—

BENJAMIN: He's gone.

ELI: I'm sorry, it'll happen to us all…the things we've seen…a Toronto boy?

BENJAMIN: He lived here most of his life. He came over from Poland.

ELI: Carried his family to freedom.

BENJAMIN: Yes, barefoot.

ELI: What?

BENJAMIN: My zadie happened to carry his family to freedom with no shoes on.

ELI: They came, they came and they took.

BENJAMIN: Oh no the Nazis didn't take them, he got out before the war. He lost them.

ELI: Lost his shoes? How?

BENJAMIN: To a straight flush.

ELI: Cards?

BENJAMIN: Yes.

ELI: Your zadie lost his shoes to a card game in Poland?

BENJAMIN: That's right.

ELI: And do you have it?

BENJAMIN: Sorry? The shoes?

ELI: The thing.

BENJAMIN: The…?

ELI: The curse.

BENJAMIN: The service is over. I should really get…

ELI:	Jus a minute! Your father's busy fixing noses for dollars, your zadia al'vesholem's praying to pull an inside straight up there...the big card game in the...they're busy. So let me—pretend I'm the goyishe thing behind the curtain. What's your sin?
BENJAMIN:	I haven't committed...it's nothing really, I just...I walk by here everyday on my way to work and this morning, this morning I decided to stop.
ELI:	Why?
BENJAMIN:	I don't know.
ELI:	Accch! Try again.
BENJAMIN:	OK. To...to talk to God.
ELI:	You haven't called him in fifteen years you think he's going to pick up first ring?
BENJAMIN:	You don't think he's listening?
ELI:	I think in case he's giving you the appropriate guilt for a week or two, you'd better run it by old Eli.
BENJAMIN:	Who?
ELI:	The prophet Eli. *(He extends a hand.)*
BENJAMIN:	Benjamin.
ELI:	Why are you here?
BENJAMIN:	You're a prophet?
ELI:	What are you doing here?
BENJAMIN:	You're...excuse me for saying this but...you're being a bit pushy.
ELI:	If we weren't pushy we wouldn't have Israel. Now, what?
BENJAMIN:	I have to go.

ELI: You can't! You can't walk out there not knowing.
                You stopped, you stopped for a reason. You walked
                in, you walked in for reason. You're still here, for
                a reason. I don't want it to be another fifteen years
                before I see you again, Boo.

BENJAMIN: What?

ELI: I know that unless you should get an answer here
                today—

BENJAMIN: You just called me Boo.

ELI: So what? Ben, Boo...you look like a Boo, not a
                Jewish Boo, mind you but—

BENJAMIN: My girlfriend calls me Boo.

ELI: She a Jewish girl? Boo?

BENJAMIN: Don't call me that.

ELI: Is it about her?

BENJAMIN: This is ridic...this really doesn't concern you.

ELI: It does.

BENJAMIN: Well, it shouldn't.

ELI: Well, it does.

BENJAMIN: Look, I'm sorry—it's not...it's just...God, this is...
                No wonder people stop coming here... This is...
                I...I'm sorry I have to —

ELI: What is it boytshik? You look terrible. Sit down a
                minute. Sit down! What have you got already?
                What?! The same as your zadie?

                Pause.

ELI: And you need money?

                Pause.

ELI: Of course you do! Why else would you be at shul?
                Everybody here's looking for... You people never
                heard of a bank?! You owe? How much?

BENJAMIN: Three thousand dollars and a trip to Mexico that
                now I don't...I don't....

ELI: You don't what?

BENJAMIN: That I don't have the money to... There I said it.

ELI: And your father the doctor can't help you?

BENJAMIN: I called him...I'm hoping—

ELI: Hoping? What hoping? He's a doctor in America,
                he's got more money than Moses.

BENJAMIN: Yeah, but it doesn't skip a generation.

ELI: What?

BENJAMIN: The thing.

ELI: G'vald. And what about your girlfriend? She don't
                work?

BENJAMIN: No, she's... This past year she got really sick.

ELI: Not a good year.

BENJAMIN: No, not...and through it all I've been...I mean I
                have been... It's the one thing I do that's just for me,
                y'know? It's the only way I can forget about it all for
                a while and just—

ELI: God knows, sometimes we need distractions.

BENJAMIN: Yeah, well lately God and me don't seem to be
                picking the same team.

ELI: Is that what you came to ask him for? A winner?

BENJAMIN: I guess. A way out, maybe.

ELI: Who'd you bet on?

BENJAMIN:	The Argos.
ELI:	Sorry?
BENJAMIN:	The Argos.
ELI:	The...? Boytshik, the Almighty himself, Noah and a couple of the key rabbis all came down joined hands and danced a hora at midfield...the Argos still couldn't put a point on the board.
BENJAMIN:	Thanks. Where were you yesterday?
ELI:	I was here.
BENJAMIN:	It shouldn't be... She hasn't been responding to her treatment and she believes that this place...that this is the place and she, she, she—
ELI:	She she she she she. A mentsh miz akhting gab'n af zayn eygener kroyt eyder er misht zikh arayn in yenems.
BENJAMIN:	Sorry?
ELI:	A man must tend to his own cabbage before giving a hand with someone else's. *(Pause.)* It sounds much better in Yiddish.
BENJAMIN:	What does it mean?
ELI:	It means there are certain things that are yours with your girlfriend, things that you came to together, yes. And then there are other things that are your own, deep down things that came by way of Poland and until you...until you take care of these things, these things which are your own, as much as you may work your little fingers in the dirt, you cannot even truly begin to help her with her cabbage.

Beat.

BENJAMIN:	I have to go.
ELI:	Rob a bank?

BENJAMIN: No, I'm...I'm going to work.

ELI: What do you do?

BENJAMIN: I'm a waiter.

ELI: It's going to have to be a helluva day in tips to—

BENJAMIN: Right...well... *(Moves to exit.)*

ELI: Wait! Take this. *(He hands BENJAMIN his tallis.)* And take a look at Master Paul's Dream, he's running Friday in the fifth.

BENJAMIN: What?

ELI: What what? I'm a prophet not a saint.

BENJAMIN: You go to the racetrack?

ELI: Since before you were born.

BENJAMIN: Jesus Christ!

ELI: Different prophet, not nearly as gifted.

BENJAMIN: Master Paul's Dream?

ELI: They're all babies, but he's worked like a house on fire.

BENJAMIN: I can't take this. *(Moves to hand him back the tallis.)*

ELI: Why not?

BENJAMIN: I don't know.

ELI: Yes! You do now. Everyman should have a tallis, Boo, for mazel.

Scene 3

A Diner. Wednesday lunch.

> BETH, 30, sits alone at a four-seat table. She has a glass of draft beer in front of her; she raises it to herself.

BETH: To...me. *(She drinks and then feigns interest in the menu.)*

> LILY, a woman in her late twenties, enters the restaurant out of breath. She is wearing a fall jacket and sunglasses. She spots BETH and moves towards her.

BETH: Here we go.

LILY: *(Reaching the table.)* Beth.

BETH: Lily.

LILY: There was a delay on the subway.

BETH: Ruth's not here yet either.

LILY: Is there a waiter?

BETH: He just—

LILY: Did you pick this place?

BETH: Yes, we were here—

LILY: Why do they call it the "Forties" diner?

BETH: Because...what do you mean? Because it's dinery.

LILY: Yes, but why celebrate the Forties?

BETH: Why not?

LILY: Oh, I don't know...war, Depression, not a lot of chicken fingers being eaten.

BETH:	It's just a restaurant.
LILY:	And who needs a menu this big?
BETH:	I don't—
LILY:	I feel like I'm in Smurf Village. Do you know why she called this?
BETH:	No, she wouldn't say over the phone.
LILY:	I hope she's—
BETH:	She's fine, I'm sure she's fine.
LILY:	She didn't sound so fine. I don't know why we just didn't go to her place.
BETH:	She wanted to try to get out. Can I buy you a beer?
LILY:	No, just a mineral water.
BETH:	Passing on the afternoon beer. Are you growing up on me or something?
LILY:	No, it's just—
BETH:	You're making me celebrate on my own.
LILY:	Oh, that's right, I heard, I'd heard you won.
BETH:	We did.
LILY:	Well congratulations.
BETH:	Thank you.
LILY:	The best in all of Ontario and you fucking won!
BETH:	The guy by the juke box didn't quite catch that.
LILY:	What? I'm not allowed to be proud?
BETH:	You're proud?
LILY:	Did I say that?

BETH: No, it's just—it's not over yet. We've got the Nationals this weekend in Regina.

LILY: The best in the country.

BETH: Not yet we're not.

LILY: Right. Well, I won't jinx it. *(Taking off her sunglasses.)* I hope there's something vegetarian on this fucking Neanderthal menu.

BETH: I saw a tofu something.

LILY: Good. I am starving.

BETH: Are you high?

LILY: What?

BETH: Your eyes are all red.

LILY: Really? *(Checks her reflection in her sunglasses.)* Must be allergies.

BETH: It's November.

LILY: I must be reacting to all this Betty Boop shit.

BETH: You're high!

LILY: The guy by the *Casablanca* poster didn't quite—

BETH: I can't believe you…that shit is going to fry—

LILY: Shit? Sh…?! Do you know the Rastafarians hold that "shit," as you call it, as a sacrament.

BETH: You're not a Rastafarian.

LILY: To them it's like the body of Christ thing.

BETH: You can't compare—

LILY: A tightly-rolled joint *or* a piece of cardboard cracker placed on your tongue by the stubby fingers of a man who's been playing with himself for the past thirty years, you're right there's really no comparison.

BETH: That is the most ridic… I can't believe you're—

LILY: I'm not! I stopped! You want me to piss in a…? I stopped.

BETH: When? Around the same time you became a vegetarian?

LILY: What's that supposed to mean?

BETH: It means, the last time we came here, the last time I saw you…my birth…July…you absolutely loved this place and the menus and you ordered a banquet burger.

LILY: I have never been here before in my life.

BETH: *(In a bad Jamaican accent.)* Oh yes you have mon!

LILY: Yeah, well…I must've blocked it out. Anyway, sober, it's fucking horrible.

BETH: So, you're actually straight?

LILY: Christ, it is the same goddamn song every time we try to—

BETH: No, you're right, far be it from me to live your life, have a… Do you know what you're going to have?

LILY: I may try the Hitler burger.

BETH: Lily. Here's the tofu surprise thing.

LILY: You know it's just like tofu.

BETH: What?

LILY: Marijuana, it's just like tofu, it can be whatever you want it to be.

Pause.

BETH: I can't believe you got high for this.

LILY: That's it. *(She gets up and grabs her coat. RUTH enters the restaurant walking slowly, in obvious pain.)*

BETH: What are you...? *(Spotting RUTH.)* Ruth's here. *(Calling and waving.)* Ruthie! *(To LILY.)* Sit down.

LILY: No way.

BETH: Sit—

LILY: It's fucking pointless.

BETH: Please—

LILY: I will not sit here and be accused—

RUTH: *(Reaches the table.)* Where are you going?

LILY: To put money in my meter.

RUTH: You don't have a car.

LILY: Don't you start with me too! I need air. My eyes are red, Miss Marple, because I've been crying! *(LILY exits the restaurant.)*

RUTH: What's going on?

BETH: I have no idea.

RUTH: I can't believe...I can't be five minutes late.

BETH: She lies so effortlessly.

RUTH: I have to go get her.

BETH: No, it's freezing out... You're not walking around out there to indulge—

RUTH: I need both of you—

BETH: How long have you known her? She'll be back. She's hungry and I'm buying.

RUTH: Right.

BETH: Can I buy you a juice or—?

RUTH: No, just water.

BETH: This celebrating alone is for the birds.

RUTH: Oh shit.

BETH: It's OK. She forgot, too.

RUTH: Congratulations.

BETH: Thank you.

RUTH: Did you get my message?

BETH: Yes.

RUTH: I wish I could've… Who was there to see it?

BETH: Who…sorry…what?

RUTH: Who? Sean and—?

BETH: He wasn't there.

RUTH: He wasn't there!?

BETH: It was in Belleville.

RUTH: So what?

BETH: So, he's got a thing about small towns.

RUTH: He's got a thing about everything.

BETH: He gets into a small town and he feels like everyone is staring at him.

RUTH: Yes, well maybe if he wasn't such a depressive…maybe if he removed the "Hello my name is Nietzsche" nametag people wouldn't stare.

BETH: They can't all be as good as Benjamin.

RUTH: I can't believe he didn't… Could you imagine what would happen to him if something actually ever really happened to him?

BETH: Don't wish that please.

             LILY re-enters the restaurant.

RUTH: *(To BETH.)* Be nice please. *(To LILY.)* Did you get a ticket?

LILY: All right, I have something to tell you both.

RUTH: That's funny, so do I.

BETH: Yes, please let's get our priorities…Ruth asked us to lunch and made the trek out here to—

LILY: I'm sorry Roo, but I won't be able to concentrate on your thing until I get this off my chest.

RUTH: A…OK.

BETH: Unbelievable.

LILY: OK. I was going to wait until after the retreat and—

RUTH: What retreat?

LILY: —and until Benji and whatisname were here but since I have been forced to prove my innocence before the appetizer, I've decided to tell you now. OK here it is…I can't believe I'm actually… All right I'm…here it goes. What is the one thing that I have wanted more than anything my entire life?

             Pause.

BETH: Curly hair?

LILY: No.

RUTH: Those Australian boots?

LILY: No!

BETH: I give up.

LILY: Jesus.

RUTH: What?

LILY: Baby.

BETH: What?

LILY: Baby.

RUTH: Baby?

LILY: Baby. *(Beat.)* I'm going to have a baby and we're going to be a Buddhist.

BETH: Buddhist?

RUTH: Baby?

LILY: And my eyes are red because I've been crying with happiness since I found out.

RUTH: What about your ovaries?!

BETH: The waiter didn't quite catch—

LILY: I know. One in a million.

BETH: Buddhist?

LILY: Yes, it's something I've been considering for a while. I'm leaving on a week-long retreat on Friday.

BETH: Friday? What about the bank?

LILY: The bank? I quit the bank a month ago.

BETH: You quit? Did you know she quit? *(Beat.)* Whose is it?

LILY: I knew you'd react like this.

BETH: Like what?

LILY: Like…Christ, can't you just be happy for me?

BETH: I am happy. I'm just happily in need of a mild sedative.

LILY: You know there are some things that happen, they just happen—things—that even you can't control.

RUTH: What are you talking about?

RUTH: Lily—

LILY: No, I am so sick of…you turn your back on everything you can't control. Your life is like this bubble that—

BETH: That's funny I don't remember ordering the psychobabble.

RUTH: OK. That's—

LILY: You know it must get pretty lonely living all alone there in that perfect world.

BETH: Perfect? Where do you get…? My life is far from perfect, Lily.

RUTH: She lives with Hamlet.

LILY: Name one thing in your life that isn't exactly where you want it to be.

BETH: How can you ask me that with Ruthie sitting—

RUTH: What? I'm the imperfection in your life?

BETH: That's not what I'm saying.

LILY: What are you saying?

BETH: I'm saying—

LILY: When Ruthie got sick you couldn't understand it.

BETH: You're fucking right I couldn't!

LILY: When Mom died the same thing—

BETH: Here we go.

LILY: You just put on your see-what-you-want-to-see blinders and you say everything is going to be all right and you know what? Sometimes, sometimes it isn't.

BETH: You don't think I know that?

RUTH: Can we stop this?!

LILY: Name one thing that's wrong with your life.

BETH: I don't have to sit here and prove to you that there are problems in my life!

RUTH: Beth.

BETH: In fact, I don't have to sit here at all. *(She gets up from the table.)*

LILY: That's right. What you can't control, you leave.

BETH: Fuck you, Buddha!

RUTH: All right—

BETH: No, not this week I can't...I won't let her...I have come too far to have my focus...I won't let you... *(To RUTH.)* Call me. Oh, and to answer your question about what could possibly be wrong with my life...ah fuck it! You don't deserve to know.

RUTH: Beth... *(She exits.)* Oh...shit.

LILY: I'm sorry Ruthie, usually I would sit here and take it, I can handle her y'know, it's just that well—now it's not just me I have to worry about.

Scene 4

A phone booth.

> *BENJAMIN stands in a phone booth. The following is heard in voice over.*

V.O.:   You have one new message. First message. *(JACOB's voice.)* Hi Benjamin, it's your daddy. I got your message yesterday and I'm sorry I didn't call you right back, honey, but things at the clinic have been—well, you know same old story: building boobs for bored Bostonians. Anyway, sweetheart, you weren't totally clear in your message about what was going on—but then you didn't really have to be. It's amazing. You and I have the exact same voice when we're broke. And—ah, anyway…I'm… We just redecorated the clinic so things are pretty tied up and I…I'm not going to have any real cash until the middle of next month. I'm sorry that I can't get you earlier kid, and ah…if you talk to your mother, don't mention…I don't have to tell you—she'll worry.

I've got an office full of patients, honey, so I should probably go and make us some money. Send Ruth my love. I love you. *(Dial tone.)*

V.O.:   End of message. Goodbye.

Scene 5

A Coffee shop.

> *BENJAMIN and BEAR, 31, approach an elevated two-seat table in an upscale coffee shop.*

BEAR: So she goes to me like this...the fucking doctor says to her if the Chicken wasn't on jazz he would've died for sure. Imagine that eh? Heroin saved the Chicken's life.

BENJAMIN: Yes, but if he wasn't on heroin, would he have been stabbed in the first place?

BEAR: That's a good point, Freud. So, then—fuck—then she goes to me...this fucking Maureen—

BENJAMIN: Who's Maureen?

BEAR: Chicken's wife.

BENJAMIN: You're all named after animals.

BEAR: What?

BENJAMIN: He's Chicken, you're Bear.

BEAR: Yes, haven't I told you that story?

BENJAMIN: No.

BEAR: There was a Chinese year-of-the-whatever calendar in Dragon's boarding room, the room we used to *(gestures his arm)* convene in. I was born in '68, Year of the Bear, Chicken was the Chicken and so forth.

BENJAMIN: There is no Year of the Bear is there?

BEAR: What are you? Chinese?

BENJAMIN: No, I used to go out with this girl who...it doesn't matter, look I need to—

BEAR: All right, it was a fucking buffalo, but who wants to be called Buffalo? Can I finish my other story?

BENJAMIN: Actually, I—

BEAR: So, then she goes to me like...she goes...she has the balls to go, are you ready for? She goes to me, if Tony wasn't with—

BENJAMIN: Who's Tony?

BEAR: Chicken!

BENJAMIN: Can you sit down please?

BEAR: After my fuckin' story. So, she goes to me like this, if Tony wasn't with you he would've never been busted or cut, you're bad luck. Me! You've seen me at the races Freud I may be a lot of fucking things but bad luck is not one of them.

BENJAMIN: You've had some nice hits.

BEAR: You're fucking right I...it's Chicken who's... He lost his father's fish store, only been in the family forty fucking years. He lost his car, lost his fucking teeth, I go to him...I go...in the holding cell I go, Chicken, if I lost the fish store and my teeth and I had a fucking wife like Maureen sitting eating Vachon cakes at home, I would commit suicide. Honest to fucking God, I would swallow Shopper's Drug Mart and end this nightmare of a life you're living.

BENJAMIN: And?

BEAR: He's thinking about it. (Laughs, beat.) What's wrong with you?

BENJAMIN: What?

BEAR: That's a funny story.

BENJAMIN: Can you sit down please?

BEAR:	Yeah, fuck. You all right, Freud? You sounded like shit on the phone.
BENJAMIN:	I'm—
BEAR:	I know why you're depressed, it's this fucking place, it's fucking depressing. What'sa matter with Tim Horny's?
BENJAMIN:	It's nicer here.
BEAR:	Nicer? Ni…I had to take out a small mortgage to pay for this coffee slushy, whatever the fuck this is. Why didn't you tell me to meet you at a bar?
BENJAMIN:	You can't drink!
BEAR:	Right…shit—right, I'm still getting used to this.
BENJAMIN:	But you're still…?
BEAR:	Twenty-three days. *(He crosses himself.)*
BENJAMIN:	Congratulations.
BEAR:	Thank you thank you, it's fucking killing me but thank you. Christ, y'know this might…I think this is the first time we've ever met outside the races.
BENJAMIN:	Yeah.
BEAR:	So, this is what I have to get used to, eh? The clean crowd.
BENJAMIN:	Bear, we need to talk.
BEAR:	The fuck we been doing?
BENJAMIN:	I need to ask you something.
BEAR:	About Lizzy?
BENJAMIN:	Who?
BEAR:	Who, your girlfriend's sister who.

BENJAMIN:	Lily!
BEAR:	Yes, what did I say?
BENJAMIN:	How was the date?
BEAR:	Fine.
BENJAMIN:	Bear?
BEAR:	It was nice, fuck.
BENJAMIN:	Nice? You didn't even remember her name?
BEAR:	It was over a month ago! I haven't had a drink in twenty-three days, I'm lucky to remember my fucking pants in the morning!
BENJAMIN:	But everything went all right?
BEAR:	Yeah.
BENJAMIN:	Because I went out on a limb for you.
BEAR:	Where'd you call me from?
BENJAMIN:	What?
BEAR:	To meet you here?
BENJAMIN:	A payphone.
BEAR:	From the track?
BENJAMIN:	What?
BEAR:	Did you go earlier? Is that why you're upset?
BENJAMIN:	No.
BEAR:	No you didn't go, or no that's not why you're upset?
BENJAMIN:	I didn't go.
BEAR:	Bullshit, how'd you do?

BENJAMIN: I didn't—

BEAR: How'd you—

BENJAMIN: I didn't—

BEAR: How—?

BENJAMIN: I was at synagogue!

BEAR: That bad huh? That's OK, even if I was still going…which I'm not! I couldn't have gone today anyway, I was down at the clinic this morning picking up my (pulls a few bottles of methadone from his jacket pocket) magic methadone. You know the biggest problem with quitting everything at the same time? I'm having a fuck of a time deciding what I miss the most.

BENJAMIN: Can you put those away please?

BEAR: Yeah, fuck…what's? You're as white as the sugar, fuck.

BENJAMIN: I need you to return for the Lily favour.

BEAR: I wish I could, Freud, but I haven't got a pot to piss in. I've got thirty-six dollars to my name. Sobriety is costing me a fortune.

BENJAMIN: It's not money.

BEAR: Nothing illegal.

BENJAMIN: What?

BEAR: I can't. You can't ask me to do nothing illegal.

BENJAMIN: It's not…Bear, I'm in trouble.

BEAR: With Wilson?

BENJAMIN: Yes.

BEAR: Did you pay your mark?

BENJAMIN: I did.

BEAR: Good. He is not a man you want to owe money to.

BENJAMIN: —and then I tried to win it back.

BEAR: What?! When?

BENJAMIN: Last night.

BEAR: And?

BENJAMIN looks away.

BEAR: Oh, shit, Freud. You were clear. The fuck d'you—?

BENJAMIN: I couldn't let him beat...the clinic's maxed out her credit card, she's paying for the plane tickets with the last of her cash, I'm covering everything else.

BEAR: So?

BENJAMIN: So, after I paid Wilson what I owed I was tapped.

BEAR: You couldn't fake it?

BENJAMIN: Yeah, sure until she asked me to buy her an orange juice at the airport and—

BEAR: So you're in to Wilson for money you don't have?

BENJAMIN: That's right.

BEAR: How much?

BENJAMIN: Three large.

BEAR: And you don't have any money for the trip?

BENJAMIN: Ah...seventy-eight dollars last time I checked.

BEAR: Fuck, Freud, this is not—

BENJAMIN: I know. I know. But, I...I've got a tip.

BEAR: A what?

BENJAMIN: A horse.

BEAR: Jesus.

BENJAMIN: Bear—

BEAR: From?

BENJAMIN: A guy.

BEAR: A guy?

BENJAMIN: I'm going to make one more bet.

BEAR: Where are you getting the money to make a bet?

BENJAMIN: That's not your concern. He's running Friday, and after we win…and this is it, so help me fucking God, we are getting on a plane to Mexico Friday night.

BEAR: Me and you?

BENJAMIN: Me and Ruth!

BEAR: How much you going to bet?

BENJAMIN: Enough.

BEAR: How much?

BENJAMIN: Enough.

BEAR: Enough is not a number.

BENJAMIN: Enough to give you three hundred.

BEAR: That's a number. You're going to give me three hundred dollars?

BENJAMIN: When we…yes.

BEAR: Christ, you're a dreamer, Freud.

BENJAMIN: Yeah, well—it's why you gave me the name.

BEAR: Anybody who bets fifty to win on a nine-year-old maiden is seriously damaged goods.

BENJAMIN: Bear listen to…I need to know if you're in on this.

BEAR: In on…? How can I be on something I don't know what the fuck I'm going in on?

BENJAMIN: After we win this, we are going away.

BEAR: Fine…fuck, have a nice trip. What's the three C for? Looking after the cat?

BENJAMIN: No.

BEAR: Clearing the walk?

BENJAMIN: Bear?!

BEAR: What?

BENJAMIN: Can you get a car?

BEAR: Yeah sure…a license may be a tad more difficult but…what? You need a lift somewhere?

BENJAMIN: The airport.

BEAR: Sure! Why didn't you just…no, fuck…I can't—shit, I'm sorry Freud, I can't.

BENJAMIN: What?!

BEAR: I can't drive with a suspended license, it'd be fucking up…I can't…I can't put myself into any danger zones.

BENJAMIN: Danger zones? You'd be driving a friend to the airport, Bear, it doesn't really fall into the danger zone, it's barely even illegal.

BEAR: What? Driving with a suspended license?

BENJAMIN: Yeah.

BEAR: No, last time I checked, all jazzed up and I drove through the front window of some pie shop, it was real illegal. I'm sorry, Freud, I can't.

BENJAMIN: When you have a suspended sentence what does that mean?

BEAR: What?

BENJAMIN: A suspended sentence.

BEAR: That you don't have to serve it.

BENJAMIN: So?

BEAR: So?

BENJAMIN: So, if your license is suspended then shouldn't that also mean that you don't have to serve the suspension?

BEAR: Fuck. Where were you when I was in court?

BENJAMIN: What do you say?

BEAR: Very convincing counsel, but I'm sorry. I can't. I can't take the risk.

BENJAMIN: It's a pretty small risk to—

BEAR: Any risk in this fragile time.

BENJAMIN: Fragile?

BEAR: Change the walk, change the talk. I'm just one of them now.

BENJAMIN: Yeah, well any one of them would take this offer.

BEAR: Any one of them aren't on probation.

BENJAMIN: It's three hundred dollars for a twenty-minute drive.

BEAR: Why don't you save yourself the three bills and take a cab?

BENJAMIN: I enjoy your company.

BEAR:	What's the real reason?
BENJAMIN:	Before the actual drive—
BEAR:	Oh, Here we go! Didn't I mention, before the actual drive you have to stab three Korean businessmen, stick a bag of jazz up your ass and cross the border dressed as a private school girl but then...THEN we just need a lift to the airport.
BENJAMIN:	You just have to buy me some time.
BEAR:	What?
BENJAMIN:	The fifth goes off at four.
BEAR:	I know when the fifth goes off.
BENJAMIN:	The flight leaves seven thirty. I'm going to have to go to the track make the bet, watch it run, collect—
BEAR:	Actually win the race goes before collect but...go on.
BENJAMIN:	Hop in a cab, pick up the tickets and then come home, where you'll be waiting with Ruth.
BEAR:	If you're already in a cab why don't you just take it right to the airport?
BENJAMIN:	No, it's not the drive. It's...she's going to be going nuts if I'm not home after work.
BEAR:	So be home after work.
BENJAMIN:	I'm going to be at the track. But if there's someone there, someone calming her...assuring her...
BEAR:	Me?
BENJAMIN:	—that there was an emergency just come up at the restaurant but that I'm going to be home in plenty of time.
BEAR:	I don't work with you.

BENJAMIN: She thinks you do.

BEAR: What?!

BENJAMIN: What was I going to tell her, Bear? I've got this great
            guy for your sister, we met in the bar at Woodbine,
            making a side bet on a photo finish—

BEAR: Which I won.

BENJAMIN: Yes, that's not...congratu...look...I can't...

BEAR: What's my vocation?

BENJAMIN: What?

BEAR: At your work, what do I do?

BENJAMIN: I didn't specify! Look, I can't have her calling work
            or coming to look for me.

BEAR: And all I have to do is?

BENJAMIN: Distract her...keep everything calm until my call.

BEAR: Your call?

BENJAMIN: Yes, I'll call right after the race, and as soon as she
            picks up the phone I'll hang up.

BEAR: Hang up?

BENJAMIN: When you don't hear her talking, you'll know that
            we've won and that I'm on my way.

BEAR: And if we lose?

BENJAMIN: If we lose? Then...then I'll talk to her...you'll hear
            her talking and you'll make up some excuse about
            getting something from the car and you'll get out of
            there, no harm no foul.

BEAR: If you lose are you coming clear?

BENJAMIN: Yes, I'll have to. So, are you in?

BEAR: I don't...I don't fucking...you've been to hell and back with this girl, Freud, why don't you just tell her, tell her you fucked up. You can't afford the trip. You fucked away your savings, you're in way over your head. I mean I know twenty-three days clean doesn't make me a fucking counselor or nothing but maybe it's just time to come clear.

BENJAMIN: I can't. I promised her this. This is not just some trip. This is her fucking life, Bear!

BEAR: You never thought of that before?

BENJAMIN: What? Oh, don't, don't, don't do this to me, Bear please, OK, because I can't...I can't—

BEAR: Why me?

BENJAMIN: What?

BEAR: Well, I think "calming influence," Bear is not the first name that pops into my head. Why me?

BENJAMIN: The truth?

BEAR: It couldn't hurt.

BENJAMIN: You're the only person I know who I thought might accept.

BEAR: And why would I do that?

BENJAMIN: I can think of three hundred reasons. Besides, it's not something for nothing. Bear, you owe me—

BEAR: I promised myself in that holding cell, no more, no more of this fucking—

BENJAMIN: The same holding cell where you told the Chicken that you would kill yourself if you ever sunk as low as him?

BEAR: Yeah.

BENJAMIN: Well, how far away from that are you, Bear? You've got what? Thirty bucks in your sock…how long before you are back in that boarding room sticking dirty—

BEAR: I'm not going back to that!

BENJAMIN: I'm not saying—

BEAR: You're comparing me to the Chicken!

BENJAMIN: No, I'm…you know how proud I am that you're doing this, but give yourself a chance to stay clean. It's three hundred dollars for a few minutes of talk and a lift to the airport. It is the easiest money you'll ever see.

BEAR: Possibly see. If we lose, I get shit.

BENJAMIN: Yeah, well, look at it this way, this way you get to gamble without actually having to gamble, right?

BEAR: Guarantee me fifty and I'll do it.

BENJAMIN: What?

BEAR: Fifty bucks guaranteed. I get the car but you drive it…that way I'm not putting my ass on the line.

BENJAMIN: OK. Yes—you're on. *(BENJAMIN and BEAR shake on it and BEAR doesn't release.)* What?

BEAR: Fifty bucks.

BENJAMIN: What, now?

BEAR: Yes now.

BENJAMIN: You…I don't…I don't have it.

BEAR gets up from the table, moves to exit.

BENJAMIN: Bear?!

BEAR: I'm sorry, Freud.

BENJAMIN: Bear? *(He continues to walk.)* Shit. Wait! *(BEAR turns,*

BENJAMIN reaches into his pocket and pulls out some money, then searches through his change.) Here.

BEAR: All right. All right. Keep your fucking change. *(BEAR takes the money and puts it in his pocket.)* I won't be no fucking Chicken. *(Pause, some swanky coffee shop jazz plays.)* I've got to get out of here, this place is enough to cause a relapse. *(Turns to exit.)*

BENJAMIN: Bear? *(BEAR turns back.)* Thanks.

BEAR: Yeah, yeah, yeah. Just win the fucking bet!

He exits. The lights fade on BENJAMIN.

Scene 6

Benjamin and Ruth's apartment. Wednesday evening.

BENJAMIN enters the apartment singing. RUTH is lying on the living room floor.

BENJAMIN: Ruth?

RUTH: I'm going to throw up.

BENJAMIN: Come on, my voice isn't that bad.

RUTH: No, I'm going to throw up.

BENAJMIN: Jesus. Ruthie?

RUTH: I lay down here because it was cold and now I can't get up.

BENJAMIN: I knew you shouldn't have gone out.

RUTH: Yeah, and would you believe they didn't even let me tell them.

BENJAMIN: What?

RUTH: I couldn't...I can't do this anymore.

BENJAMIN: Yes, you can! And when this is all over I swear I am
             going to fly you to the moon, Ruth Rocket.

RUTH: I'll settle for Mexico.

BENJAMIN: You're on.

RUTH: Boo?

BENJAMIN: Yeah.

RUTH: Don't watch. *(She dry heaves and nothing comes out.)*
             Oh, fuck.

BENJAMIN: Let me get you to bed.

RUTH: What if I don't make it back?

BENJAMIN: What?

RUTH: I know that's why I haven't been able to tell
             them...I don't want to say goodbye because...
             because what if I say goodbye and then
             it's...goodbye...and how do you prepare—?

BENJAMIN: We are coming back, Ruth!

RUTH: And if I don't?

BENJAMIN: What?

RUTH: Where will you bury me?

BENJAMIN: Ruth!

RUTH: I guess the obvious would be beside Mom but...I
             don't know, where would you choose?

BENJAMIN: I don't...I don't know. I don't want to talk about
             this.

RUTH: OK. I'll get back to you on it, though.

BENJAMIN: Yeah, in about seventy years. Get into bed. I'm
             going to get you some water and then—

RUTH: And then you'll call them?

BENJAMIN: What?

RUTH: Don't tell either one that the other one is coming, but tell them both the same time. Tomorrow night...I can't say this more than once.

BENJAMIN: We're going to get better, Ruth.

RUTH: Yeah.

BENJAMIN: I love you.

RUTH: Make the call, OK?

> *RUTH exits. BENJAMIN looks at her money that sits in an envelope on a small table. He moves to the table, grabs the wad of money. He pulls the tallis out of his pocket. There is a lighting change. DR. JACOB ROTH, a man in his late thirties, enters.*

JACOB: Benjamin.

BENJAMIN: Dad. Finally.

JACOB: How was it?

BENJAMIN: Is that a trick question?

JACOB: I know it's terrible, but it's important.

BENJAMIN: Why?

JACOB: You're Jewish.

BENJAMIN: So?

JACOB: So, your bar mitzvah's in less than two months and from what I hear you could use the lessons.

> *JACOB holds out a twenty-dollar bill.*

BENJAMIN: What's that for?

JACOB: What? You've never taken a pay-off before? Every

58 ZADIE'S SHOES

time you finish a lesson you get one of those, just until your bar mitzvah and then you can do like every other good Jewish boy and never step foot in there again.

BENJAMIN: Amen. Where's the car?

JACOB: A couple of blocks.

BENJAMIN: Should we take a cab to the car?

JACOB: Yeah, give me my twenty back and I'll hail one. Wiseguy.

BENJAMIN: Are we going to Bub's for dinner?

JACOB: No, your Bub's not feeling great so I thought we'd try this other place I know. It's my favourite restaurant.

BENJAMIN: Not the House of Chan?

JACOB: No, it's in the west end. It's got this kind of oval design. It smells like horseshit but...

BENJAMIN: Yeah?

JACOB: Yeah, why not?

BENJAMIN: Is Mom...?

JACOB: I told her it was boys' night out.

BENJAMIN: Does she know we're going?

JACOB: I think I might've forgot to mention it.

BENJAMIN: She'll smell smoke in my hair.

JACOB: You worry too much, Benjamin.

BENJAMIN: I just...I don't know...I'm not sure.

JACOB: You're not sure?

BENJAMIN: If...to have to...if we have to lie—

JACOB: Who said anything about lying?

BENJAMIN: I'm not sure we should go Dad.

JACOB: So, so we won't go.

                Pause.

BENJAMIN: Are you upset?

JACOB: No, I just thought...we've both been working so
                hard—l thought we could go have some fun, that's
                all.

BENJAMIN: I'm sorry.

JACOB: We'll catch an early show or something... *(Peeling a
                hundred bucks off a wad of twenties.)* Here...this is
                yours.

BENJAMIN: What?

JACOB: It's a charley. I got it out for you to play with but...
                Here, take it, I got it for you.

BENJAMIN: I don't...thank you. *(Looking down at the money and
                then to his dad.)*

JACOB: Put half in your back pocket.

BENJAMIN: What?

JACOB: Always put half in your back pocket, sweetheart.

BENJAMIN: *(BENJAMIN does so.)* Dad?

JACOB: Yeah?

BENJAMIN: Would we have gone to the clubhouse?

JACOB: We'd have to eat, right?

BENJAMIN: Did you have reservations?

JACOB: Yeah, but I'd have gone anyway.

BENJAMIN: Very funny. Ah, we can't...I don't have a sports
              jacket.

JACOB: In the trunk.

BENJAMIN: What if she notices it's out of my closet?

JACOB: Benjamin. Listen to me for a minute. In less than
              two months you are going to be a man. You know
              my friend Morty? G.P.

BENJAMIN: Yes.

JACOB: Morty Miskin is a man, he has to pish, he asks his
              wife first. You don't want to be a wuss, Benjamin
              and you... Most of all you don't want to be the type
              of man whose friends have to worry that he's going
              to roll over on them if his wife notices a sports coat
              missing from his closet.

                    Pause.

BENJAMIN: Dad?

JACOB: Yeah.

BENJAMIN: Are we going to make post?

JACOB: If we hustle. Come on! (*JACOB runs off. Disappears.*)

BENJAMIN: Dad? Wait up. I'm coming!

RUTH: (*From off.*) Boo?!

BENJAMIN: Coming. (*BENJAMIN stuffs the tallis and money in his
              pocket and exits as the lights cross fade.*) I'm coming.

Scene 7

Beth and Sean's apartment.

> *The lights come up on SEAN, a man in his late twenties, sitting reading a book. BETH enters with her curling shoes and a cloth to polish them. There is a beat of silence at the top of the scene.*

BETH: What are you reading?

SEAN: Book.

BETH: Novel.

SEAN: No, it's a history.

BETH: No, I was saying it's novel that I ask you what you're reading and you...forget it. *(Long silence.)* Anything about King Frederick the Second in that history? Crazy bastard this Freddy. See, there was this huge debate about what language people instinctively spoke, Latin, Hebrew, Greek, or of course the one Freddy was super pulling for, German. So, Freddy gets his hands on all of these orphaned babies and has them raised in complete silence, to settle the debate.

SEAN: And?

BETH: Sorry?

SEAN: *(Looking up from his book for the first time.)* Well, what language did they end up speaking?

BETH: Oh, a...none. They all died, in silence. I need a new cloth. *(She exits.)*

SEAN: Is there something you'd like to discuss?

BETH: What's that, Freddy?

SEAN: You've been like this all night.

BETH: Like?

SEAN: Actually, you've been like this all month.

BETH: Sorry...like? *(She re-enters the room.)*

SEAN: Antagonistic.

BETH: It's just a story.

SEAN: You're always like this after you see your sisters.

BETH: I told you, this was no ordinary visit. I'm going to be an auntie.

SEAN: You can't get over the—

BETH: Get over? I just found out the woman who hasn't done her taxes in nine years is going to be a mother.

SEAN: Yeah, well...at least someone's getting some. *(SEAN goes back to his book. Silence.)*

BETH: How many times do we have to do this?

SEAN: Once more would be good.

BETH: I am riding an unbelievable streak of luck and I will not do anything to risk—

SEAN: Yes, I've heard. It will change your luck. It will change the energy you play with. But have you given a single thought to how it has changed our relationship?

BETH: It shouldn't change...maybe... You know maybe that speaks volumes about our relationship, if a few weeks of celibacy changes things so—

SEAN: Yes, you know what it says about our relationship? It says that one of the participants in the relationship likes having sex, very much! And when he's not having it, when he is forced to sit on the couch night after night reading about the Crimean War and railing at the injustice that is—

BETH:	You rail even when you're having sex.
SEAN:	Yes, but there's a softness to it.
BETH:	What if I got in an accident?
SEAN:	What?
BETH:	Christopher Reeves falls off a horse and now his wife—
SEAN:	Oh, can we leave Superman out of this, please? He has nothing to do with this.
BETH:	He has everything to do with this.
SEAN:	OK. You know what, if I were him… Yes, if I were him I would've used that respirator tube and blown myself into the pool a long time ago. But I am not him and I am also not you! Which is why I still fail to see any connection between what goes on in our bed and your success in the curling rink.
BETH:	What goes on in our bed—
SEAN:	Not much lately.
BETH:	Luck goes in streaks and if you do anything to disrupt the streak, anything different from when the streak began, you run the risk—
SEAN:	Wait, wait—so you're saying that had we made love that night of your first win at the Metros when all of this started, that right now we would be—
BETH:	Humpin' like monkeys!
SEAN:	I had a cold!
BETH:	C'est la vie.
SEAN:	That is possibly the most ludicrous—
BETH:	It goes in streaks. You would know that if you…ah I don't know why I am still trying to explain this to

you, you who have never competed a day in your life. You wouldn't know a streak if it jumped up and bit you on the ass, so please, don't begin to tell me that it doesn't run in streaks.

SEAN: Not only does "it" not run in streaks but "it" doesn't exist! Luck? It's just another way for people to try to explain why horrible things happen. Your little sister gets cancer—is that because she's unlucky? No, it's because her white blood cells started to mutate at an astronomical...it's because your mother also had cancer. Everybody walks around saying "my luck has got to change," bullshit! Maybe you've got to change, maybe everything has got to change. Maybe that salt you're throwing over your shoulder, for "luck," is landing in someone else's eye. Maybe it's landing in a lake raising the saline levels and killing all the fish. But as long as *my* luck doesn't change right? As long as I can hang on for just one more day without something horrible happening to *me*, then salt in the eye and dead fish and cancer, oh well, these are just things that happen to unlucky people!

Pause.

BETH: What the fuck are you talking about?

SEAN: Luck.

BETH: No, you're talking about your dick.

SEAN: My unlucky dick.

BETH: No, you're talking about me not being able to make a choice in this...you're talking about playing everything by your rules.

SEAN: My rules? You've made so many rules I can't even move in here anymore.

BETH: You need serious help, Sean.

SEAN:	This coming from a woman who sweeps ice for a living.
BETH:	You know, maybe, maybe you're right. Maybe this streak has nothing to do with why I don't want to sleep with you.
SEAN:	Now we're talking.
BETH:	Maybe...
SEAN:	What? *(The telephone rings.)* Leave it.
BETH:	I can't.
SEAN:	Beth.
BETH:	I can't...I can't, it's probably Ruth.

The phone continues to ring as the lights crossfade.

Scene 8

Benjamin and Ruth's apartment.

BENJAMIN enters and answers the phone.

BENJAMIN:	Hello. How did you get my number? I can't talk right now. I und...yes I under...I understand that. I'm just...no...no of course n... *(There is a sound from offstage.)* I've...yes...I've just... You'll have the money tomorrow. *(He hangs up and RUTH enters.)*
RUTH:	Who was it?
BENJAMIN:	Nobody...just...the restaurant.
RUTH:	Do they want you to go back in?
BENJAMIN:	I wish.
RUTH:	That's nice.

BENJAMIN: Well this is…it's fucking absurd.

RUTH: What would you like me to do, Boo? You knew they were coming over. *You* called them.

BENJAMIN: I can't believe they didn't let you tell them yesterday.

RUTH: Welcome to my world.

BENJAMIN: Selfish. Selfish—

RUTH: Hey, they're my sisters.

BENJAMIN: And they're selfish.

RUTH: What happened today?

BENJAMIN: What?

RUTH: Did someone order butter on their corned beef sandwich or something?

BENJAMIN: Yeah, that's right…my job is a joke. I mean how could there be any real stress in a job that technically a really smart sponge could perform? I'm actually a writer y'know. A writer who hasn't written a word in almost a year but—

RUTH: It was a joke.

BENJAMIN: That's OK, so is my writing career.

RUTH: Is that my fault?

BENJAMIN: Is that what I said?

RUTH: That's what you're implying.

BENJAMIN: I'm not implying… Look maybe I should just go out and let you do this on your own.

RUTH: Do and I'm not taking you to Mexico. Give me the tickets.

BENJAMIN: Umm….

RUTH: The tickets.

BENJAMIN: I couldn't get out of work. I'm going to get them tomorrow.

RUTH: We leave tomorrow!

BENJAMIN: Perfect timing.

RUTH: Benjamin!

BENJAMIN: What? I called the guy…they're sitting on his desk. I'm going to get them first thing in the morning.

RUTH: Why do you always have to wait until the last possible moment to do everything?

BENJAMIN: I'm not the only one.

RUTH: You're picking up plane tickets; I'm dealing with the Borgia sisters.

BENJAMIN: I didn't know it was a contest.

RUTH: It's not. Can we…can we stop this please? I'm sorry they're on their way over. I'm sorry I didn't tell them yesterday. Lily kind of stole the show.

BENJAMIN: When doesn't she steal the—?

RUTH: She's going to have a baby.

BENJAMIN: What?!

RUTH: I didn't tell you yesterday. I knew you'd freak.

BENJAMIN: She's pregnant?!

RUTH: Yes.

BENJAMIN: Whose—?

RUTH: Who knows—

BENJAMIN: Jesus.

RUTH: —I mean you know Lily, she's a one-woman dating game, so it could be any number of—

BENJAMIN: Oh God.

RUTH: —so you see it was kind of… She's going to have a baby.

BENJAMIN: Yeah, well you are trying to have a life!

RUTH: Don't yell at me. I didn't want to rain on her parade all right, not that…I mean Beth took care of that pretty quickly.

BENJMAIN: Miss Practicality.

RUTH: What's the matter with practicality?

BENJAMIN: Nothing, if you're looking for a mini-van but in a person it can get a bit—

RUTH: You sound just like your father. You're not like your father.

BENJAMIN: What's wrong with my father?

RUTH: Nothing. I love your father but you're not like him—

BENJAMIN: Yes I am.

RUTH: OK. You know what I'm going to… *(She moves to exit.)*

BENJAMIN: Don't just walk out on this.

RUTH: Walk out on…what am I walking out on?

BENJAMIN: We're always avoiding things.

RUTH: Who's avoiding what?

BENJAMIN: I can't just keep dancing around this.

RUTH: Dancing around what? What are you talking about?

BENJAMIN: Don't get mad at me.

RUTH: Oh, right...what have I got to get mad about? You're the one that had the shitty day.

BENJAMIN: Ruthie.

RUTH: Don't make this about you.

BENJAMIN: I'm not, but there's something—

RUTH: It's one more day.

BENJAMIN: Ruth—

RUTH: One more day. Don't lose it on me now.

BENJAMIN: I'm tired. I'm sorry... I'm just so fucking tired.

RUTH: Come here. You are my knight. You are. You are my knight in wholesale armour.

BENJAMIN: Yeah, I don't know what's wrong with me.

RUTH: *(She hugs him and feels the tallis in his jacket pocket.)* What's this?

BENJAMIN: A...a tallis. *(Pulling it out of his jacket, it falls to the ground and the prayer book falls out.)* And a prayer book.

RUTH: Where did you get them?

BENJAMIN: I picked them up.

RUTH: You couldn't pick up the plane tickets, but you had time to go tallis shopping?

BENJAMIN: I stopped by B'eth Jacob yesterday on my way to work. I'm thinking about maybe starting to go again.

RUTH: To...?

BENJAMIN: Yes.

RUTH: OK. I'll take all the help I can get. You should kiss it.

BENJAMIN: What?

RUTH: It touched the floor. Your father once told me, anything Jewish touches the floor, you kiss it. *(BENJAMIN kisses the tallis and puts it around his neck.)* Very nice. Now how about me?

                 BENJAMIN moves to RUTH and then lifts up an end of the tallis for her to kiss. She laughs, kisses it.

BENJAMIN: I'm sorry.

RUTH: *(Grabbing the tallis and pulling him closer with it, they kiss.)* Everything's going to be OK, Boo.

BENJAMIN: You think?

RUTH: We just need to get out of here, that's all.

BENJAMIN: Yeah.

                 They kiss again and then RUTH breaks the embrace.

RUTH: They're going to be here any minute. I should put on my fatigues.

BENJAMIN: They're your sisters Ruth. They're going to understand.

                 RUTH exits. BENJAMIN puts the money back in the envelope.

Scene 9

Benjamin and Ruth's apartment.

LILY:	*(To BENJAMIN.)* You told me she wasn't going to be here!
BENJAMIN:	I lied.
BETH:	Well, this was very mature.
BENJAMIN:	I heard yesterday afternoon was a lesson in maturity.
BETH:	You realize I leave in a few hours?
RUTH:	Yes.
BETH:	And that I do have things…important things to do.
LILY:	Me too.
BETH:	Of course! The Amish.
LILY:	Buddhists.
BETH:	Right, the Amish were last year.
LILY:	They were Quakers.
BETH:	I'm playing for the national championship in less than forty-eight hours and I'm arguing religion with Reverend Cannabis.
LILY:	You're so—lost to yourself.
BETH:	And you're a fucking idiot.
RUTH:	Stop. Right now…both of you! Stop and sit down and shut up for three seconds, please!
BETH:	Ruthie—
BENJAMIN:	Let her.

RUTH: I don't have the energy to...I tried to do this... I've
            been trying to do this...

LILY: What?

RUTH: You're not the only ones going away.

BETH: What?

RUTH: We're going away too.

BETH: What are you talking about?

RUTH: We leave tomorrow night.

LILY: Where to?

RUTH: Mexico.

BENJAMIN: A clinic in Mexico.

BETH: A clinic?

RUTH: A treatment clinic.

BETH: You're being treated here.

RUTH: Not any more.

BETH: What?!

RUTH: I ordered them to stop.

BETH: You what?

LILY: How long are you going for?

RUTH: A few months. I've got to fight this a different way.

BETH: What, with voodoo?

RUTH: It's not voodoo.

BETH: I don't believe this.

RUTH: This is something I have to do.

BETH:	You can't be serious *(To BENJAMIN.)* How could you let her —?!
BENJAMIN:	I—
RUTH:	This was my call.
BETH:	And what have your doctors said about this?
RUTH:	They really don't have much to say, what with all the good their poisons have been doing. *(To LILY.)* Worked wonders for Mom too, didn't they?
BETH:	You're not Mom!
RUTH:	No, I'm not! And I'm definitely not gunning for the same results.
BETH:	This is insane.
RUTH:	No, actually this is the most sane thing I've done in a long time.
BENJAMIN:	You know the doctors…most of her doctors have managed to swallow their pride and wish her luck.
BETH:	Luck? Wonderful.
BENJAMIN:	It would be nice if you could…
BETH:	Well, I can't…I'm sorry…she's not their sister!
RUTH:	I don't expect you to understand.
BETH:	Good because I can't…I can't fucking believe this.
RUTH:	But if you care about me—
BETH:	If? God, Ruthie…I care more than…more than…
LILY:	More than winning gold?
BETH:	You… *(She steps towards LILY.)*
RUTH:	Don't! This…Mexico…this is what I need.

BETH:	No, I can't believe that the advances of Mexican medicine are what you need.
RUTH:	So, don't! I don't care. I can't...I didn't bring you here to argue this. I needed to say goodbye, so, goodbye... I said it. Goodbye.
BETH:	Ruth.
RUTH:	Goodbye.
BETH:	No, it's not that easy... Can we please talk about this?
RUTH:	Talk? You don't... We don't talk.
BETH:	You can't just drop this on me and then...can you please just postpone this...just until I get back and we can sit down and—?
RUTH:	No!
BETH:	Ruth—
RUTH:	Goodbye.
BETH:	Ruthie.
RUTH:	I don't want to hear another word. Tomorrow. Tomorrow we are off!

There is the sound of a bell going off and the racing gates opening. Followed by the sound of horses charging out of the starting gate.

TRACK
ANNOUNCER: And they're off!

BENJAMIN is in a spotlight. He takes the money from the envelope, and the sound of horses running continues as the lights fade to black.

End of Act One

Act Two

Scene 1

Friday.

A spotlight rises on RUTH.

RUTH: *(Prayer book in hand.)* The hufftorah. This ought to
            kill some time. *(Flipping through it.)* The Book of
            Ruth. Sounds like a good one.

            A spotlight rises on BETH.

BETH: The Lord is my shepherd I shall not want. He
            maketh me lie down in green pastures. He leadeth
            me to...shit! This is not my style! Practicing makes
            more sense then praying. I need to win this. To win
            this goddamn thing, just...win. And I know I
            should only be praying for Ruthie but...I have
            worked too hard and sacrificed too much to get this
            close and not... I've got to have this! I have to! Do
            you hear me?

            A spotlight rises on LILY.

LILY: Buddha? I know I'm supposed to pray to you in
            silence, but I've read a lot of books and joined a lot
            of groups...and I don't really feel like I'm in a
            position to risk leaving anyone out so...ah...what is
            it they always do on Muchmusic, Buddha? A shout
            out. I'd like to do a shout out, I think. OK, um...so,
            I guess I'll just...shouting out to Yahweh and Jesus.
            To Vishnu and Shiva. To Mother Earth and Allah.

To you my main man Buddha. To Alpha and
Omega, Jehovah and Jah. To Bumba and Mama-
choka. To Rama, Yama, Istar, the boyz on Olympus,
my girlfriend goddesses. Health. For my sister.
And my baby.

A spotlight rises on BEAR.

BEAR: Hello my name is Bear. I am an alcoholic heroin-
addicted gambleholic...is there a limit on these?
No? Good. And I've been clean for twenty-five
days.

RUTH: And Ruth said, "Urge me not to leave you. For
wherever you go I will go. Wherever you lodge, I
will lodge. Where you die, I will die, and there will
I be buried.

A spot comes up on ELI.

ELI: There was a man who prayed to God for a winner.
In a bathroom stall...looking up in between
races...and he goes, "God, I have nothing in the
world but this twenty-dollar bill... please... save
my life, send me down a winner. And all of a
sudden the bathroom opens up...the ceiling starts
to crack with the light and the thing and the big
booming voice of God comes through the...and
goes, "Noble Concorde" And the man goes "Noble
Concorde? Noble Concorde is thirty-six-to-one."
And God turns to Moses and goes, "Everybody's
an expert." And the man goes, "No, I'm sorry, it's
just... I lose this last twenty and that's it, I've got no
reason left to live so...are you sure?" And God
goes, "Am I sure? Shmuck, I will reach down with
my big glorious omnipotent hand to where this
horse is being saddled in the paddock and I will
touch with my huge glowing perfect hand this
horse on the nose and I will say...as I said to Moses
here, I will say 'Noble Concorde, COME FORTH!'"

The lights come up on BENJAMIN sitting on the
bench behind ELI at the synagogue.

BENJAMIN: And?

ELI: The horse ran fifth. *(Waits for the laugh, doesn't get it.)*
              Get it? Come forth...ran fifth... Achh, it's an old
              one. So, you're back?

BENJAMIN: Yeah, I couldn't....

ELI: Shul twice in three days.

BENJAMIN: What can I say? I'm hooked.

ELI: Nice tallis.

BENJAMIN: Thank you.

ELI: *(Referring to his tallis.)* My back-up. It's a bit of a
              shmata but—

BENJAMIN: I should give you this back.

ELI: Someday. When you're rich and famous. *(Beat.)*
              You look worried, boytshik.

BENJAMIN: Master Paul's Dream opened at seventeen-to-one.

ELI: So?

BENJAMIN: So, that worries me.

ELI: How do you think he feels?

BENJAMIN: I don't care how he feels.

ELI: He's the one got to run.

BENJAMIN: I've got more at stake.

ELI: I see. So you came back to make absolute about the
              tip. You've been walking around wondering who
              was this meshugene gave me this horse anyway—?

BENJAMIN: It's not you.

ELI: —he walks with a thing. *(Referring to his hearing aid.)* He wears a thing for his thing. Maybe his kop is about as good as his hearing. Maybe he meant to give me the five-to-two shot picked in every paper. Maybe he got confused. Maybe, maybe the only reason I gave you the horse was so that you'd come back to shul... What a place, go put in a couple hours and come out with a winner. *This* is a place I would go every Saturday.

BENJAMIN: You gave me the horse so I'd come back to shul?!

ELI: It worked, didn't it?

BENJAMIN: I knew...it was just a con.

ELI: Praying to God is not a con!

BENJAMIN: Oh my...What am I? I need a miracle.

ELI: So ask. You're here already, what the hell, ask. How many of our prayers do you think actually make it up there? There's about fifteen of us alte kakers come here every morning to pray. How many of our prayers do you think actually make it all the way to the big shooter? What are *our* odds? I'm asking.

BENJAMIN: I don't care.

ELI: That's right. Who cares to one! Those are our odds. And "who cares" is something much different than "I don't know." "Who cares" is an "I don't know but I'm still going to choose to *do* something!" Believe in something. Now, Master Paul he doesn't know he's seventeen-to-one. What does he know? He knows he woke up this morning ate some oats, had a kuk and later maybe he'll go for a run with a few friends. That's what he knows! He doesn't know the odds and he don't care, he's still he's going to show up, try his best. We don't know the odds and we don't care, we still show up, try our best. Faith boytshik. And will this horse win? Perhaps. And will I go to heaven? Perhaps. But either way you've got to start believing in something…showing some goddamn faith in something sometime. Make the bet, don't make the bet, but either way you've got to tell her.

BENJAMIN: What?

ELI: Win or lose, boytshik, you've got to tell her the truth. It's the only way to start taking care of some of them cabbages.

BENJAMIN: You gave me a bullshit tip.

ELI: It's not a bullshit tip.

BENJAMIN: It's not a…? You just told me—

ELI: What did I tell you?

BENJAMIN: The only reason you gave me the tip was so that I'd come back to shul.

ELI: A test. Prophets, we test. That's what we do.

BENJAMIN: Eli?

ELI: Yes, Boo.

BENJAMIN: Do you actually have a tip on this horse?

ELI: Actually …. yes.

BENJAMIN: From who?

ELI: Would you believe the sky opened up?

BENJAMIN: No.

ELI: Sam Green.

BENJAMIN: Who?

ELI: Sammy Green. He's a boyfriend of mine from the lodge. He's a hotwalker. Spends more time with these horses than he does with his wife. He says the horse can't lose.

BENJAMIN: You're leaving?

ELI: The service is over.

BENJAMIN: The fifth doesn't go off until four.

ELI: Yes, fortunately I know something I can do there while I'm waiting. You coming?

BENJAMIN: I'm...I'm shaking.

ELI: There's nothing to shake about, Boo, it's just a horse race. *(BENJAMIN doesn't move.)* A couple days ago we couldn't get him in here, now we can't get him to leave.

BENJAMIN: I can't...I need a minute. *(BENJAMIN sits staring straight ahead, ELI watches him for a beat.)*

ELI: You know there was this Hassidic boy, he asked his Rabbi, he said "Rebe, what should one do as a preparation for prayer?" And do you know what the Rabbi answered, boytshik? "Pray!" I'll be in the parking lot. *(He exits.)*

BENJAMIN: Dad? I'm going down. Please...help me. Put your arms around me and lift me up and over the turnstile with a form in my pocket and this prayer on my lips: please God, let me break even. Please bring home this winner, one time.

Scene 2

The racetrack/the curling rink.

TRACK
ANNOUNCER: As the horses parade on to the track for the fifth race on today's card, this twelve-thousand dollar claiming event for two-year-old maidens is set to go six furlongs over the main track. The track is listed as good. Seven minutes. Seven minutes to post time.

SPORTSCASTER: Final end, last rock, we're all tied at seven. Beth Rocket needs a clean draw inside the eight-foot to move Ontario through to the second round. It all comes down to this—

BENJAMIN: Give me a thou…eight hundred to win on the four. Yes, the four! Give me a $2 part wheel the four all-all. Give me a fifty-dollar exactor box the 1-4. A thirty-dollar 3-4. Box. A forty-dollar box, the 4-9. The total? Eleven…OK. *(Peels the money off.)* Thank you—

SPORTSCASTER: Thank you, Colleen. You know she's made this shot a million times in the practice rink and now she's… *(With whispered intensity.)* Here we go, Rocket stares down the ice. Look at the intensity in those eyes, Colleen… She rocks into motion and—

TRACK
ANNOUNCER: *(There is the sound of the bell, the gates opening, horses charging out.)* They're off. Dance Me Gently broke well. Along side of that one is favourite Blitzer. To his inside tucked in third is Pookyvision with HurlyBurly back in fourth. It's two lengths back of that one to Sleezewaltz, Nanabana is back in sixth, beside him is Road of War. Roofraiser is back in eighth, Mario's machine is ninth, and as they hit the first turn the early trailer is Master Paul's Dream.

SPORTSCASTER: Clean release, Colleen. But she...she may have come up a bit early on it... It looks like she might have been a bit shy with the weight, they're going to have to really get on this and—

TRACK
ANNOUNCER: As they hit the eight pole it's still Dance Me Gently, Dance Me Gently and Blitzer, three lengths back to Nanabana who's done his best running and is now packing it in on the rail. It's one length back of that one to long-shot Master Paul's Dream, who's made a huge move from the back of the pack to be fourth. It's Dance Me Gently, Dance Me Gently and Blitzer who's beginning to tire to his inside. It's Dance Me Gently. Dance Me Gently by two as Blitzer continues to fade. It's Dance Me Gently, Dance Me Gen...and *here comes* Master Paul's Dream!

BENJAMIN: Come on with this, Master Paul! Come on with this four.

TRACK
ANNOUNCER: Who's finding his best stride and absolutely flying down the middle of the racetrack—

BENJAMIN: Keep him rolling!

BETH: Hurry! Hurry! Hard! Hurry!

BENJAMIN: One time with this fucking four!

SPORTSCASTER: I don't know if its got enough on it, Colleen, it's— it's going to be real close...

TRACK
ANNOUNCER: With three furlongs left to go it's Dance Me Gently, Dance Me Gently two lengths in front of a charging Master Paul who's taken over second but may run out of real estate. Dance Me Gently, it's Dance Me Gently and Master Paul now closing to within one.

BENJAMIN: One time!

BETH: Hard!

TRACK
ANNOUNCER: It's Dance Me Gently, Dance Me Gently fighting gamely to hang on, it's Dance Me Gently and Master Paul now within half a... It's Dance Me Gently, Dance Me Gently and Master Paul closing with every stride...

BENJAMIN: Go...get there...

TRACK
ANNOUNCER: They're neck-and-neck as they come to the wire it's...

SPORTSCASTER: Oh my...I can't believe it, Colleen, in all my days I've never, she's—she's...

TRACK
ANNOUNCER: Too close to call! A photo for win between Dance Me Gently and Master Paul's Dream. Running time was 104 flat. What a fabulous finish by the eager two-year-olds, this one is for the judges to decide as they'll examine a photo to win between Dance Me Gently and late-charging long-shot Master Paul's Dream. Please hold all your tickets.

> *Crossfade to BENJAMIN and RUTH's apartment.*

Scene 3

Benjamin and Ruth's apartment.

> *There is a loud and hurried knock, there are two large packed suitcases by the door ready to go.*

RUTH: Who is it?

BEAR: Bear.

RUTH: Who?

BEAR:	Bear! I'm a friend of Freud's.
RUTH:	Freud?
BEAR:	Ben.
RUTH:	Bear?
BEAR:	I'm a friend of Bear's!
RUTH:	What?!
BEAR:	Shit. Ben's! I'm driving you to the airport.
RUTH:	Oh. God, I'm…*(RUTH opens the door.)* I'm sorry. I'm a bit distr…I was just watching my sister… where's Benjamin?
BEAR:	Has he called?
RUTH:	What?
BEAR:	He hasn't called?
RUTH:	I'm sorry—?
BEAR:	The phone. It hasn't rang?
RUTH:	No, not recently. Why?
BEAR:	Recently how?
RUTH:	Where's Benjamin?
BEAR:	When was the last time it rang?
RUTH:	What?
BEAR:	The phone.
RUTH:	I don't… He told me you were coming together.
BEAR:	The lobsters got out.
RUTH:	What?!
BEAR:	The tank got broke… Some kid forgot to take his

Ritalin I guess, and I feel just sick about it, I mean they're my lobsters.

RUTH: Sorry?

BEAR: I supply the restaurant with all their fish. I run a very successful fish store, it's how I met Freud.

RUTH: Freud?

BEAR: That's what I call Ben.

RUTH: So, he's still at work—?

BEAR: He should be here any minute.

RUTH: Has he got the tickets?!

BEAR: Not to my knowledge... Yes.

RUTH: I'm going to call him. *(She exits off to get the phone.)*

BEAR: *(Calling after her.)* You can but they won't answer...they're knee-deep in crustaceans... Look, he sent me over here ahead because he knew you'd be anxious. *(RUTH enters with a portable phone in her hand.)* I was supposed to be here twenty minutes ago but this fucking car was not waiting for me like it was supposed to be—anyway, I'm here now and you've got nothing to worry about, we're going to get you to the airport in plenty of time.

RUTH: It's rush hour.

BEAR: So, when he gets here, we'll rush.

RUTH: It's busy. *(Beat.)* I can't believe he stayed—

BEAR: You know Freud, he felt responsible, it happening on his shift.

RUTH: Yeah, well he's going to feel a lot more than responsible if we miss this plane.

BEAR: Ah, do you mind if I? *(Motions to sit.)*

RUTH: Yes, of course, I'm sorry I'm being a terrible host, can I get you beer or something?

BEAR: Tha'd be great.

           RUTH moves to exit.

BEAR: Wait!

RUTH: What?

BEAR: I can't.

RUTH: You can't?

BEAR: I can't drink. I mean I can, I just—can't...now. See, I have a couple beer, wake up with a headache, take a few Tylenol 3 to get rid of the headache, and the next thing you know I'm selling the fish store for jazz.

RUTH: So, no beer?

BEAR: I'd better not.

RUTH: I can't believe this.

BEAR: You look good.

RUTH: Sorry?

BEAR: My old man died of cancer...throat...and in the end it was like—well it was like that hole in his throat just got bigger and bigger and eventually just swallowed the poor fuck alive.

RUTH: I'm sorry.

BEAR: But you look real...I mean if you weren't already taken I'd... At least I got to keep it in the family.

RUTH: Oh that's right...you're the...Lily.

BEAR: Yeah. She's pretty great.

RUTH: She's all yours. Actually I've got another one too, if you want.

BEAR: You're not close?

RUTH: Not lately.

BEAR: It's hard on a family.

RUTH: Sorry?

BEAR: Cancer. And people always react in a totally different way than you think they're going to.

RUTH: Tell me about it. *(Silence.)* This is…sorry but something's not right. We should drive down and get him?

BEAR: Give him a minute. Great place.

RUTH: Thank you.

BEAR: Spotless.

RUTH: When I'm anxious I clean. It runs in my family. We used to say when my mother got really stressed that she'd head straight for the bottle…of Pledge. *(Beat.)* Sorry, you've been here three minutes and I'm already talking about my mother.

BEAR: I don't mind. Is she gone?

RUTH: Yeah, she died when I was twelve.

BEAR: Of…?

RUTH: The same thing I've got.

BEAR: My mom's gone too.

RUTH: I'm sorry.

BEAR: So is the L.C.B.O.

RUTH: What?

BEAR: Replace your mom's bottle of Pledge with a quart of
             Gordon's Lemon Gin and you've got my mom.

RUTH: Oh God, I'm sorry I didn't mean to… Open mouth
             insert foot.

BEAR: I do it all the time.

RUTH: Were you two close?

BEAR: Yeah. During happy hour. *(They share a laugh. There
             is a knock at the door.)* Phone?

RUTH: Door. *(RUTH moving to it.)* Boo?

LILY: Ruthie? It's me.

RUTH: Lily?

BEAR: Lily, shit. *(Preps himself.)*

             RUTH opens the door and LILY enters the room.

RUTH: What are you doing here?

LILY: I need to talk to you.

BEAR: Hello stranger.

LILY: Bear! What are you —?

RUTH: He's driving us to the airport. We're leaving.

LILY: I know. I needed to see you before you left. And
             you…I was just about to call you.

BEAR: Right on.

LILY: I've had a lot on my mind.

BEAR: I've had you on mine.

RUTH: Did you watch Beth?

LILY: What?

RUTH: It just ended. She lost. First round.

LILY:	What?!
RUTH:	It came down to the last shot. Her last shot and she blew it. Totally my fault, I'm sure. You must be thrilled—
LILY:	I'm not. Bear, could you give me a minute with my sister.
BEAR:	What?
LILY:	Could you wait in the other room for a minute?
RUTH:	Lily.
BEAR:	I need to be by the phone.
RUTH:	Why?
BEAR:	If he calls.
RUTH:	Why would he call?
BEAR:	He won't, I mean I'm sure he's…it's just if he…in case he…I'm very worried about the lobster!
RUTH:	That's it! We're going down there right now.
BEAR:	A minute.
RUTH:	No, no more minutes
LILY:	Ruth?
RUTH:	What?!
LILY:	I need to… *(Motions to talk to her in private.)*
RUTH:	No. We're leaving. Bear?
BEAR:	Ah—
LILY:	Please… *(She takes RUTH by the arm and leads her away from BEAR.)*
RUTH:	I don't believe this… This is beyond selfish.

LILY: I'm coming with you.

RUTH: What?

LILY: I know I drive you crazy, but we can't be apart while you're going through this, and I'm going through this and I've still got some of my Mom fund left so…I've booked a flight out for tomorrow.

RUTH: No! I'm sorry Lil, but this is something Benjamin and I have to do… just the two of us.

LILY: I have to come. And I have to tell him.

RUTH: What?

LILY: I come, he's here. It's a sign. I have to tell him—

RUTH: Tell him what?

LILY: He's the… *(Touches her belly.)*

RUTH: Oh my… We will deal with this later, all right?

LILY: No, it's a sign. He's obviously here for a reason.

RUTH: Yes, to drive us to the airport.

LILY: Well, I have to tell him before we go.

RUTH: Go where?

LILY: To Mexico.

RUTH: You're not going to Mexico.

LILY: Bear?

RUTH: Lily.

BEAR: You rang?

LILY: I need—

RUTH: No, he'll freak… We'll lose our drive.

LILY: He's not like that.

RUTH: You've known him for ten hours!

LILY: Bear—

RUTH: Don't!

BEAR: What is it?

LILY: I'm—

             The telephone rings. They all look at it. BEAR and RUTH look at each other. They both dive for the phone. BEAR realizes that she should be answering it and steps back.

RUTH: Hello? *(Beat.)* Hello? Hello? They hung up.

BEAR: Fucking A!

             Blackout.

Scene 4

The racetrack.

             BENJAMIN running from the wicket through the grandstand with a wad of cash in his hand, on his way to the exit. ELI is sitting on a bench outside, BENJAMIN spots him.

TRACK
ANNOUNCER: Six minutes to race six, six minutes.

BENJAMIN: Eli! Where were you? I went up to bet and I lost you.

ELI: I was in a bathroom stall praying for a winner.

BENJAMIN: Well, we got one. Did you see that?!

ELI: I saw.

BENJAMIN: I had him all—all.

ELI: What did the tri pay?

BENJAMIN: Forty-eight hundred and eight on the nose.

ELI: The total.

BENJAMIN: Almost fourteen thousand.

ELI: Good boy. Sit down a minute.

BENJAMIN: I'd love to Eli, but I've got a plane to catch.

ELI: You're going on vacation? Good for you. Boston?

BENJAMIN: No.

ELI: Vegas?

BENJAMIN: Eli—

ELI: Don't tell me you're going to Poland to buy your zaida's shoes back.

BENJAMIN: We're going to Mexico.

ELI: We?

BENJAMIN: My girlfriend and—

ELI: I see.

BENJAMIN: What?

ELI: You're not going to tell her.

BENJAMIN: Tell her…?

ELI: You can take my tip, but not my advice.

BENJAMIN: What are you talking about?

ELI: You didn't hear a word I said except the name of the horse.

BENJAMIN: I heard—

ELI: A man must tend to his own cabbage before giving a hand with someone else's! What do you suppose that means?

BENJAMIN: I don't have time for... What time is it?

TRACK
ANNOUNCER: Five minutes to race six. Five minutes.

ELI: I'm down four hundred dollars, that's what time it is.

BENJAMIN: What?! What about Master Paul?

ELI: I loved the six in the third.

BENJAMIN: You didn't bet on Master Paul?!

ELI: What was I suppose to bet him with?!

BENJAMIN: Oh, Jesus, I...I didn't realize you'd blown your...you should've said something...well... *(He peels several bills of his wad.)* Here.

ELI: What's this?

BENJAMIN: What? You've never taken a pay-off before?

ELI: I don't want your money.

BENJAMIN: This way it'll be like you had him.

ELI: You still don't—

BENJAMIN: Don't be...you saved my...take it.

ELI: A man must tend to his own cabbage—

BENJAMIN: Forget the cabbage!

ELI: That's right. *(He grabs the money.)* Forget it! *(He throws the money on the ground.)*

BENJAMIN: What are you...? *(Goes to pick up the money.)*

ELI: *(Moving to the money, stepping on it and grinding it into the pavement.)* Leave it! It's not what this is about.

BENJAMIN: You're crazy.

ELI: Name me a prophet they haven't called crazy and
             I'll eat my yarmulke.

BENJAMIN: You're not a prophet, Eli! You're a...

ELI: A what? Say it. A what? A bum?!

BENJAMIN: I didn't—

ELI: Eli Shifman is a bum! Eli Shifman is a bum!

BENJAMIN: *(Looking around.)* Eli, please...

TRACK
ANNOUNCER: Four minutes to race six. Four minutes.

ELI: Now you?

BENJAMIN: What?

ELI: What are you? Huh? Mr. Slick? What the hell are
             you?!

BENJAMIN: I'm—

ELI: To think for a second you can come here, fill your
             pockets and then drive off to your castle, the
             princess...and not tell her?!

BENJAMIN: Watch me. *(Turns to exit.)*

ELI: That's right! Go, go and show us, big shot. Show me
             and Zaid and Dad what we already know, you can't
             keep lying—

BENJAMIN: *(Turning back.)* You don't even know me!

ELI: I don't know you?

BENJAMIN: No, you—

ELI: I know that if you don't tell her the truth, you'll be
             back here in a couple of weeks throwing your shoes
             into the pot, and let me tell you something boytshik

and I pray this time you're listening. It is one thing to live this life alone, but it is quite another to put someone else's dreams...someone, unlike yourself, someone who you actually love...to place their dreams on the back of some sweaty first-time starter who's running last as they turn for home. What kind of a man would do this? Ah. *(Picks the money off the ground and shoves it into BENJAMIN's hand.)* Goodbye, Boo. I'd offer you mazel but you wouldn't know what to do with it if you got it! *(He exits, a beat.)*

TRACK
ANNOUNCER: Three minutes to race six. Three minutes.

> *Pause. BENJAMIN looks to the exit and then the money.*

BENJAMIN: *(Walks to the wicket.)* Yeah, give me three hundred to win on the three.

Scene 5

The rink. Regina.

> *BETH sits in the now-empty stands staring at the ice. SEAN enters.*

BETH: You were here?

SEAN: Yeah.

BETH: It must've cost you a fortune.

SEAN: "And for everything else there's Master Card."

BETH: Pretty small town. Regina.

SEAN: About 100,000...or that's what they say, but in the cab from the airport I saw maybe six or seven people, and I think that was only because they were frozen dead by the side of the road.

BETH: I lost.

SEAN: I saw.

BETH: I make that shot in my sleep.

SEAN: I know. I've heard you.

BETH: A clean draw inside the eight foot.

SEAN: Beth, the pressure was...I mean you had all those people with all those pins in their hats... screaming, hoping you'd miss.

BETH: And you?

SEAN: What?

BETH: What were you hoping?

SEAN: I was hoping like hell that you'd make it.

BETH: Yeah?

SEAN: Yeah.

BETH: I wanted to win—

SEAN: I know.

BETH: I wanted to win so bad because I thought that if I won and it was in the hands of the gods—

SEAN: The curling gods.

BETH: Then anything was possible. And I was going to show her that. And then she would have faith in the possibility of anything, and then no matter what they're all saying, she'd get better.

SEAN: It's—

BETH: If I win, she'll get better.

SEAN: She's going to... There's going to be a next year.

BETH: Not for me.

SEAN: What?

BETH: I'm done.

SEAN: Beth.

BETH: I'm done competing.

SEAN: You don't have to decide that right now.

BETH: I just did.

SEAN: Beth you are not going to stop playing the sport that
             you love—

BETH: No, you're right. I'm not going to stop playing...
             Actually, I'm going to *start* playing, I'm just going
             to stop competing. You?

SEAN: Huh?

BETH: Do you want to stop competing with me, Sean? Do
             you maybe just want to start playing again?

SEAN: I do.

BETH: But first I've gotta... I may be going to Mexico for a
             while.

SEAN: OK.

             Beat.

BETH: Why'd you come?

SEAN: I don't know. I woke up at like five, you weren't
             there and I...I couldn't get back to sleep. I started
             thinking about the last few weeks and how
             we've...how I've been...and I don't know. I saw
             your towel hanging off the door and a million
             different outfits piled at the foot of the bed...I could
             still feel you there and I felt...lucky.

BETH:	What?
SEAN:	I felt lucky, and I wanted to come tell you, I guess.
BETH:	So tell me.
SEAN:	I'm lucky.
BETH:	I'm a mess.
SEAN:	It's OK.
BETH:	I may be for a while. Are you going to be OK with that?
SEAN:	Of course I'll be OK with that...I'll be OK with anything...I'm getting laid tonight.

The lights crossfade up on:

Scene 6

Benjamin and Ruth's apartment.

> *BENJAMIN enters the apartment in the darkness with flowers and a bag of Chinesse food.*

BENJAMIN: Ruth? Ruthie? *(A door slams from off.)* I'm sorry, they were closed. I tried to plan everything so perfectly but I never checked what time they...they closed at five. I know I shouldn't have stayed at the restaurant but this...it's going to work out for the best. I already called the airport, flew out there in a cab and picked up *(pulls out the tickets)* a direct flight into Ixtapa, leaves eleven-forty tomorrow morning and we are on it. And not only are we on it, but we are on it first class. It's the least I could do—so, tomorrow...eleven-forty in the a.m., champagne and orange juice in those little...Ruth? I'm a horrible person I know but...we're not the first people to miss a plane. We'll have a quiet night, I got some Chinese—that soup you like. What do

	you say?
BEAR:	*(From off.)* I should fucking kill you. *(Lights up.)*
BENJAMIN:	What the fuck's goin'—Ruth?
BEAR:	Where were you?
BENJAMIN:	Ruthie?
BEAR:	She's asleep.
BENJAMIN:	Is she OK?
BEAR:	You hung up!
BENJAMIN:	What did you tell her?
BEAR:	Where were you, Freud?
BENJAMIN:	Bear. What did you tell her?
BEAR:	Where the fuck were you?
BENJAMIN:	I was on my way.
BEAR:	On your…? A whiskey-dicked geriatric monk comes faster than you did. You stayed at the track.
BENJAMIN:	What?
BEAR:	You won it! You were homefree, and you couldn't walk out of there.
BENJAMIN:	I didn't—
BEAR:	You stayed and you made another bet.
BENJAMIN:	The travel agency was closed.
BEAR:	Because you stayed at the fucking track!
BENJAMIN:	Ten minutes.
BEAR:	Fuck.
BENJAMIN:	It didn't make a differ—

BEAR: Bullshit. All you had to do was follow the fucking plan. Make the call, hang up, pick up the tickets and come home.

BENJAMIN: I was—

BEAR: Twenty minutes I waited and the next thing I know we're all on a fucking road trip to find you. She tells me to drive to the restaurant, I don't know where the fucking restaurant is—

BENJAMIN: What did you — ?

BEAR: —then she notices the baby seat in the back. I tell her it's my sister's car, my nephew's seat and we keep driving. Then I fucking sense something…I just fucking…I looked in the mirror and…cops! Three cars back.

BENJAMIN: You don't have your license.

BEAR: Not only that but my sister doesn't have a fucking kid. And not only doesn't she have a fucking kid but she doesn't have a fucking car and the one we're driving around in…I stole from the parking lot of Loblaws!

BENJAMIN: What?! You weren't suppose to—

BEAR: The fuck was I supposed to do? Buddy's car wasn't waiting for me, I was going to miss your call.

BENJAMIN: Oh my God, what—?

BEAR: I swerved onto a fucking side street and told them to get out of the car, and we stood there. We just fucking stood there. Cops circling, her plane taking off and then she…and she's been a rock through the whole thing but suddenly she…she got it, Freud.

BENJAMIN: Got what?

BEAR: She figured it out.

BENJAMIN: No.

BEAR:	You…the fucking way you've been acting, the fucking phone call… the past few days… it all comes into focus and—
BENJAMIN:	Fuck.
BEAR:	—she figured you out, Freud.
BENJAMIN:	And you?
BEAR:	I confirmed every word.
BENJAMIN:	You…!
BEAR:	Then she started to cry…right there on the fucking curb.
BENJAMIN:	How could you—? You ruined my life.
BEAR:	I ruined your…?
BENJAMIN:	You couldn't have made something up?! God, your whole life has been a series of lies, you couldn't have made up one more? To save her…to save your friend?
BEAR:	My friend? Who's my friend? Who's my fucking friend, Freud? You? You? You fucking hypocrite. You come in here and you accuse me…you accuse me, you fucking asshole, cause you don't have the balls to look in mirror and ask yourself. What the fuck are you? *(He grabs BENJAMIN.)* Who the fuck are you?
BENJAMIN:	—the fuck out of my face.
BEAR:	Not until you tell how you could do it.
BENJAMIN:	Bear let go.
BEAR:	You won, you were clear… How could you do this to her?!
BENJAMIN:	Her? Her? *(He throws BEAR to the couch.)* Fuck her?! This isn't about her. I love her. *(RUTH enters.)* This isn't about— *(Beat.)* Ruth.

RUTH: Go to Lily's now, Bear.

BEAR: I'm not leaving.

RUTH: I'm fine. I'll be… You should be with Lily now.

BEAR: Yeah. I'm part of this family now. What a fucking day. Fucking relapse written all over it. *(He exits.)*

RUTH: This was never about me.

BENJAMIN: Ruth.

RUTH: And I thought it was. I convinced myself that you were so distracted because you were worried about me.

BENJAMIN: I was—

RUTH: Because I was the thing that you loved most in this world.

BENJAMIN: You are.

RUTH: Bullshit.

BENJAMIN: Ruth.

RUTH: Tell me the truth.

BENJAMIN: The truth is the travel agency was closed.

RUTH: No.

BENJAMIN: They were closed.

RUTH: The truth.

BENJAMIN: That is the truth.

RUTH: No, the real truth.

BENJAMIN: The real truth?

RUTH: Yes.

BENJAMIN: The real…you want the real….the real truth

is…when you got sick I didn't know how to——

RUTH: Don't! Don't you…

BENJAMIN: —I didn't know how to—

RUTH: No! Don't you pin this on me. You stole my money.

BENJAMIN: I didn't steal—

RUTH: And you made a bet.

BENJAMIN: I had no choice.

RUTH: You risked my life on a horse race.

BENJAMIN: Ruth.

RUTH: And you didn't bet on the favourite, did you? *(Beat.)* Let me tell you something, Benjamin, if I die that's going to be my call. Mine. I won't let you kill me.

BENJAMIN: Ruth…we won. *(Pulling a wad of money out.)* We won. We won!

RUTH: Give me the twelve hundred dollars that you stole from me.

BENJAMIN: We've got way more than that.

RUTH: Give it to me!

             BENJAMIN hands her all the money. She takes the twelve hundred and throws the rest on the floor. She moves to exit. He gets in her way.

RUTH: Get out of my way.

BENJAMIN: Don't—

RUTH: Which part of that didn't you fucking understand? Move.

BENJAMIN: You can't just leave—

RUTH: I know now that this—us—this whole thing has
               been a lie.

BENJAMIN: It wasn't—

RUTH: But if you ever meant anything you ever said to
               me...if you ever cared—

BENJAMIN: Ruth—

RUTH: —for even a moment about me...then you will
               move out of my way and let me walk out that door.

               *After a beat BENJAMIN steps aside. RUTH grabs
               her bag and moves to the door. She opens the door
               and BENJAMIN goes to her and grabs her arm.*

RUTH: You want me to stay?

BENJAMIN: Yes.

RUTH: OK...I can stay. I can stay and we can sit up all
               night... You can sit up with me, Benjamin, and
               watch all the pain and the disappointment rip
               through every inch of...you can sit up with me,
               Benjamin, and watch while I hate your fucking
               guts. All in. You're called.

               *Beat. He looks away, she exits. He sits on the couch,
               then lies down. There is a lighting change. JACOB
               appears.*

BENJAMIN: Dad?

JACOB: It's late.

BENJAMIN: You were fighting. Is Mom—?

JACOB: She's fine.

BENJAMIN: It sounded like she was crying.

JACOB: She'll be fine.

BENJAMIN: Are you sure—?

JACOB: Relax, Benjamin. I'm sorry we woke you. Now, close your eyes.

BENJAMIN: What?

JACOB: Close your eyes, I'm going to tell you a story.

BENJAMIN: I'm not a baby.

JACOB: You're my baby. Close your eyes. Go shluf.

BENJAMIN: This is weird.

JACOB: Sha. Now, this is a story…a thing I saw once. There were these two drunks in the grandstand smoking and drinking and screaming for a two-dollar show bet you know the type?

BENJAMIN: Yeah.

JACOB: So, they both have a win bet on the seven horse.

BENJAMIN: Is he the favourite?

JACOB: No, about six-to-one. Close your eyes. So, he's leading the whole trip, but he gets caught in the last furlong by the favourite. Well, they scream bloody murder, rip up their tickets, spill their beers and then sit there for a long time in silence. Until one of them he turns to the other and he goes, "You know we may have just lost our bus fare home, Jackieboy, but I still love you." And Jackie, he goes, "No you don't, nobody loves me." But his buddy insists " I do…I really do love you." And then Jackie he grabs his buddy and he starts to shake him, then he starts to cry and he goes, "We'll see…we'll see if you really love me." And he looks his buddy square in the eyes and he goes, "If you really love me…tell me what's hurting me?" And there's a long silence and his buddy—as much as he really does love him—he can't. Your mother…she can't. I can't. I should get to bed. Goodnight, honey.

The lights fade.

Epilogue

The lights come up on ELI sitting on a bench in synagogue. BENJAMIN enters.

BENJAMIN: Eli?

ELI: Boytshik.

BENJAMIN: You don't look so good, Eli.

ELI: No? Neither do you. End of November…goddamn trotters.

BENJAMIN: Yeah.

ELI: Bishone haba b'Gulfstream.

BENJAMIN: Sorry?

ELI: Next year in Gulfstream.

BENJAMIN: Yeah, shouldn't you be in Florida?

ELI: What? I'm an old Jewish man, it's November, I have to be in Florida?

BENJAMIN: I thought they passed a law.

ELI: Wiseguy. Shouldn't you be south?

                Beat.

BENJAMIN: Do you have any family here, Eli?

ELI: I have a son… He's an architect in British Columbia.

BENJAMIN: There aren't buildings in Toronto?

ELI gives him a look.

BENJAMIN: Does he ever come to visit?

ELI: Once he came, but I'd give you even money that the
              next time he comes will be to bury me. *(Beat.)* So,
              how long has it been?

BENJAMIN: Hmm?

ELI: Since the big win.

BENJAMIN: Two weeks.

ELI: He doesn't call, he doesn't write... What have you
              been doing with all that money? *(BENJAMIN gives
              him a look.)* And?

BENJAMIN: I can't lose.

ELI: Mazel Tov.

BENJAMIN: It's driving me crazy.

ELI: So, if you've still got money, what are you doing at
              shul? *(BENJAMIN pulls a letter out of his pocket.)*
              What's this?

BENJAMIN: It came yesterday.

ELI: From?

BENJAMIN: Mexico.

              *The lights come up on the three sisters on a beach in
              Mexico. LILY is sitting in the lotus position
              drinking a coffee. BETH is taking in the sun. RUTH
              is finishing her letter.*

BETH: Is that coffee?

LILY: Yes.

BETH: You shouldn't be drinking coffee.

LILY: The child's father is Bear, Beth. I think a coffee addiction is the least of our worries. Hey, speaking of coffee, Ruthie how was the—

RUTH: Just. *(Holds out her hand meaning "Give me a minute.")*

LILY: You know I've been reading a lot about the Aztec.

BETH: I don't want to hear it.

LILY: No, they have some really interesting rituals.

BETH: You can't join the Aztecs, they're an extinct tribe.

LILY: So, I'll save a fortune on membership fees.

BETH: I think I liked you better before you got a sense of humour.

LILY: No, you didn't.

BETH: Oh, right.

RUTH: I'm... Will you tell me if this sounds stupid?

LILY: Of course she will.

BETH: Read it.

RUTH: *(Reading:)* Benjamin, I just got back from my first enema cafeina and thought of you.

BETH: Nice opening.

LILY: Very appropriate.

RUTH: I wouldn't be writing if I didn't need something from you. I just finished my first week of treatment and realized that you have something of mine. Something very precious that I'm going to need if I'm to have any real shot at surviving this. My faith. You took it from me Benjamin, and I need it back, immediately. Ruth.

The lights crossfade back to the synagogue.

ELI: G'vald.

BENJAMIN: Yeah, I got it and I...I need to... Will you?

ELI: What?

BENJAMIN: I need you to be the goyishe thing behind the curtain.

ELI: What?!

BENJAMIN: I need to confess now Eli.

ELI: To me?

BENJAMIN: I don't have anybody else.

ELI: OK. Boytshik...OK. What's your sin?

BENJAMIN: I can't let them beat me. Not like they beat him. My zadie was sixteen, just married, and trying to make a few extra bucks around the high holidays. He had a full house—kings and threes—and he lost. He lost his only pair of shoes to a straight flush. And my father...my father has spent a lifetime trying to win them back. My father thinks that if he wins enough, kicks the shit out of them, that it will erase all the pain and the embarrassment that his father's gambling caused...caused his mother...caused him. And me...I gamble to try to erase all the pain and embarrassment that my father's gambling has caused me.

             Beat.

ELI: That's not a confession.

BENJAMIN: What?

ELI: It's a history lesson.

BENJAMIN: It's not a—

ELI: You don't know how to confess and it's not because you're Jewish...it's because you're still hiding.

BENJAMIN: I'm trying.

ELI:			Try harder.

BENJAMIN:		I can't.

ELI:			Why?

BENJAMIN:		I'm scared. *(Beat.)* I'm scared. I'm so fucking scared.

ELI:			Of what?

BENJAMIN:		Of everything.

ELI:			No, of what?

BENJAMIN:		I don't know!

ELI:			Stop hiding.

BENJAMIN:		I couldn't... She gave me the chance and I couldn't...I couldn't watch her hate me. I can't have anyone hate me.

ELI:			Why?

BENJAMIN:		I need them to like me...to love me. I love her...I love her so much and this...it...I would be such a good boyfriend if I didn't...and...

ELI:			What?

BENJAMIN:		I did everything so she wouldn't see it because if she saw it...if she saw it she would leave and I'd be....

ELI:			Say it!

BENJAMIN:		It'll take over...it'll...and then no one will see how wonderful I am anymore...how much I can love. They'll just see it. I'll become it...and I'll be ugly. I'll be so fucking ugly...so dead and ugly and .... alone. I'm alone. *(He breaks down.)* How could I...? How can I... How can I get better?

			Beat.

ELI:			I don't know, boytshik. I don't know.

BENJAMIN cries harder. ELI reaches out to touch him but can't. There is a long beat of silence. When ELI's story begins it starts softly, almost to himself)

A boy is walking in the forest and he loses his way. For hours he walks with the rain and the things hitting him in the face but still he can't find a path that will lead him out of the woods. For three days he searches, and every time he thinks he's reached the edge he realizes he's only gone in deeper. Then suddenly, out of nowhere, an old man appears. An old man with the beard and the rags and no shoes on his feet. The boy sees him and runs to him, laughing and crying, "My God, you have no idea how happy I am to see you! I've been lost for three days, I thought I was going to die." And the old man he looks at the boy and goes, "How long did you say you've been lost in the woods, boytshik?" "Three days, I've been searching for a path for three days." And the old man looks at the boy and goes, "Three days? Three days? Try ten years!" The boy hears this, and bursts into tears, "When I saw you I thought that I was saved, that you would show me a path out of the woods, now I see there is no hope." And the old man he turns to the boy and he goes, "Still I can teach at least one thing of great value. I can show you all of the paths that do not lead out of the forest."

BENJAMIN reaches for ELI's hand and tentatively grabs it. ELI puts his other hand on top of BENJAMIN's as the lights fade to black.

The End